D0513966

The Delia Collection
Pork

BBC
BOOKS

Published by BBC Books
BBC Worldwide Ltd
Woodlands
80 Wood Lane
London W12 OTT

First published in 2004
Reprinted 2007

Text © Delia Smith 2004
The moral right of the author has been asserted
Design © New Crane Ltd 2004

A proportion of these recipes has been
published previously in *Delia Smith's Winter
Collection*, *Delia Smith's Summer Collection*,
Delia's How To Cook Books One, *Two* and *Three*,
*Delia Smith's Complete Illustrated Cookery
Course* and *Delia Smith's Christmas*.

All rights reserved. No part of this book may
be reproduced, stored in a retrieval system or
transmitted in any form or by any means,
including electronic, electrostatic, magnetic tape,
mechanical, photocopying, recording or otherwise
without prior permission in writing from the
copyright holder and publisher.

Edited for BBC Worldwide Ltd
by New Crane Ltd

Editor: Sarah Randell
Designer: Paul Webster
Sub-editors: Heather Cupit, Diana Galligan
Picture Editor: Diana Hughes
Recipe Testing: Pauline Curran, Sally Henley
Bren Parkins-Knight, Fiona Roberts
Commissioning Editor for the BBC: Vivien Bowler

ISBN 978 0 563 48734 0

Printed and bound in Italy
by L.E.G.O. SpA

Colour separation by Radstock Reproductions Ltd
Midsomer Norton

Cover and title page photographs: Peter Knab
For further photographic credits, see page 136

Introduction

When I look back over my years of cookery writing, I have to admit that very often, decisions about what to do have sprung from what my own particular needs are. As a very busy person who has to work, run a home and cook, I felt it was extremely useful to have, for instance, summer recipes in one book – likewise winter and Christmas, giving easy access to those specific seasons.

This, my latest venture, has come about for similar reasons. Thirty four years of recipe writing have produced literally thousands of recipes. So I now feel what would be really helpful is to create a kind of ordered library (so I don't have to rack my brains and wonder which book this or that recipe is in!). Thus, if I want to make a recipe using pork, I don't have to look through the pork sections of various books, but have the whole lot in one convenient collection.

In compiling these collections, I have chosen what I think are the best and most popular recipes and, at the same time, have added some that are completely new. It is my hope that those who have not previously tried my recipes will now have smaller collections to sample, and that those dedicated followers will appreciate an ordered library to provide easy access and a reminder of what has gone before and may have been forgotten.

Delia Smith

Author's note Pork used in this book is *British*. One very important reason for including a book specifically on pork for this collection is to promote British pork and bacon products. Firstly, because it is the finest in the world and secondly, because British farmers are struggling to survive and compete with cheaper and very often inferior imports. So please, please buy British!

Conversion Tables

All these are approximate conversions, which have either been rounded up or down. In a few recipes it has been necessary to modify them very slightly. Never mix metric and imperial measures in one recipe, stick to one system or the other.

All spoon measurements used throughout this book are level unless specified otherwise.

All butter is salted unless specified otherwise.

All recipes have been double-tested, using a standard convection oven. If you are using a fan oven, adjust the cooking temperature according to the manufacturer's handbook.

Weights	
½ oz	10 g
¾	20
1	25
1½	40
2	50
2½	60
3	75
4	110
4½	125
5	150
6	175
7	200
8	225
9	250
10	275
12	350
1 lb	450
1 lb 8 oz	700
2	900
3	1.35 kg

Volume	
2 fl oz	55 ml
3	75
5 (¼ pint)	150
10 (½ pint)	275
1 pint	570
1¼	725
1¾	1 litre
2	1.2
2½	1.5
4	2.25

Dimensions	
⅛ inch	3 mm
¼	5
½	1 cm
¾	2
1	2.5
1¼	3
1½	4
1¾	4.5
2	5
2½	6
3	7.5
3½	9
4	10
5	13
5¼	13.5
6	15
6½	16
7	18
7½	19
8	20
9	23
9½	24
10	25.5
11	28
12	30

Oven temperatures		
Gas mark 1	275°F	140°C
2	300	150
3	325	170
4	350	180
5	375	190
6	400	200
7	425	220
8	450	230
9	475	240

Contents

Roasting

Baking Grilling Frying

Loin of Pork Dijonnaise
Serves 6

about 3 lb (1.35 kg) loin of pork, chined (backbone loosened – ask the butcher to do this for you), and with the rind scored

1 tablespoon Dijon mustard

3 tablespoons fresh white breadcrumbs

1 heaped teaspoon whole peppercorns

1 dessertspoon chopped fresh sage

sea salt

For the gravy

1 dessertspoon plain flour

10 fl oz (275 ml) dry cider

salt and freshly milled black pepper

For the garnish

3 small Cox's apples

1 oz (25 g) butter

You will also need a small baking tray, and a solid roasting tin, approximately 10 x 12 inches (25.5 x 30 cm), and some kitchen foil.

Pre-heat the oven to gas mark 7, 425°F (220°C).

This has a lovely golden crust and the crackling is cooked separately to go with it. Pat the skin of the pork with kitchen paper and place the meat, uncovered, on a plate in the fridge for the skin to dry – a day or so before cooking, if possible.

Start by scoring the skin of the pork with the tip of a very sharp knife, or Stanley knife, or you can now even buy a special scalpel from a good-quality kitchen shop! Even if it is scored already, it is best to add a few more lines. What you need to do is score the skin all over into thin strips, bringing the blade of the knife about halfway through the fat beneath the skin. Then take off the skin, together with about half the layer of fat underneath – in one piece if possible. Place this on the baking tray, sprinkle generously with sea salt, then put it on the highest shelf of the oven for 20-25 minutes or until it is a very crisp and crunchy piece of crackling to accompany the meat. When you remove it from the oven, pour the fat into a bowl to use later for frying, etc.

Meantime, place the breadcrumbs in a mixing bowl. Crush the peppercorns with a pestle and mortar, or using the back of a tablespoon, and add them to the breadcrumbs, together with the sage and about $\frac{1}{2}$ teaspoon salt. Next, spread the mustard all over the layer of fat left on the pork, then press the breadcrumb mixture firmly all over, making sure that it is well coated. Transfer the joint to the roasting tin and place a square of foil lightly on top. Place the meat on a high shelf in the oven, reduce the heat to gas mark 5, 375°F (190°C), and roast the pork for about 2 hours, basting occasionally, and removing the foil for the last 30 minutes. When the pork is cooked, leave it in a warm place to relax, then spoon off the fat from the roasting tin. Sprinkle the flour into the juices in the tin and quickly work it in with a wooden spoon over direct heat. Now turn the heat up to medium and gradually add the cider, this time using a balloon whisk, until it comes up to simmering point and you have a smooth, rich gravy. Taste and season with salt and pepper.

For the garnish, core but do not peel the apples, then cut into rings and fry gently in the butter in a large frying pan until tender. Serve the pork, cut in slices, with the gravy and some crackling, garnished with the fried apple rings. New potatoes and a green vegetable would be good in summer, and in winter, roast potatoes and braised red cabbage.

Marinated Pork with Jerk Seasoning and Grilled Pineapple Salsa
Serves 6

6 large pork chops

1 large red chilli, deseeded

½ small red onion

½ tablespoon chopped fresh flat-leaf parsley

1 clove garlic, peeled

¾ inch (2 cm) piece of fresh root ginger, peeled and sliced

½ teaspoon sea salt

½ teaspoon ground allspice berries

¼ whole nutmeg, grated

⅛ teaspoon each ground cinnamon and ground cloves

juice of 1 lime

1 tablespoon Japanese soy sauce

1 tablespoon groundnut or other flavourless oil

1 tablespoon molasses sugar

10 fl oz (275 ml) dry white wine

salt and freshly milled black pepper

For the salsa

1 medium pineapple

1 tablespoon groundnut or other flavourless oil

1 tablespoon runny honey

1 small red onion, finely chopped

½ medium red chilli, deseeded and diced

juice of 1 lime

2 tablespoons chopped fresh coriander leaves

You will also need a baking tray, 11 x 16 inches (28 x 40 cm).

In the Caribbean, jerk seasoning comes either wet or dry. The latter is made with dried herbs, which I don't usually have available, so this is the wet version.

Start this way ahead of time: trim the fat off the chops and season them with salt and pepper, then place all the other ingredients, except the wine, in a food processor and mix to a thick paste. Next, spread half the paste over the base of a shallow dish, place the chops on top, then spread the rest of the paste over the surface of each chop. Now cover the dish with clingfilm and leave for a few hours to marinate, so the flavours can develop.

Meanwhile, make the salsa. For this you need to first pre-heat the grill to its highest setting, then mix the oil and honey with a good seasoning of salt and black pepper. Then, using a sharp knife, cut the top and bottom off the pineapple and, standing it upright on a chopping board, remove the skin using a large serrated knife, then dig out the 'eyes' using the tip of a potato peeler. Now cut the pineapple in half lengthways, then lay each half, cut side down, on the surface and slice each into 6 long wedges. After that, trim off the inner core. Next, brush each wedge with the honey mixture and place them on the baking tray, then pop them under the grill about 1½ inches (4 cm) from the heat and grill for 10-15 minutes, until they become nicely charred; you'll need to turn them halfway through the cooking time. After that, allow them to cool slightly before chopping roughly into ½ inch (1 cm) pieces and mixing them with the remaining salsa ingredients. Then set aside till needed.

When you're ready to cook the chops, pre-heat the grill to its highest setting for 10 minutes. Place the chops on the baking tray, making sure their surface is completely covered with the marinade (reserve the marinade left in the dish), then grill them 3 inches (7.5 cm) from the heat for about 15 minutes. After that, turn them over, spread the surface with the rest of the marinade and grill for another 15 minutes, until they are cooked and nice and crisp.

Remove them to a serving dish, then scrape any crusty bits and remaining marinade from the baking tray into a small saucepan. Add the wine, let it bubble and reduce by about a third, and pour it over the pork. Serve with the salsa.

Roast Pork with Roasted Stuffed Apples with Thyme and Parsley
Serves 8

5 lb (2.25 kg) loin of pork, chined (backbone loosened – ask the butcher to do this for you), or a piece of boneless leg of pork, either with the rind scored

1 small onion, halved

1 tablespoon sea salt

1 tablespoon plain flour

10 fl oz (275 ml) dry cider

10 fl oz (275 ml) vegetable stock (or vegetable cooking water)

salt and freshly milled black pepper

For the stuffed apples

1 lb (450 g) good-quality pork sausagemeat or sausages

8 small Cox's apples

2 teaspoons chopped fresh thyme, plus 8 small thyme sprigs

1 rounded dessertspoon chopped fresh parsley

a little melted butter

salt and freshly milled black pepper

You will also need a solid roasting tin, approximately 10 x 12 inches (25.5 x 30 cm) but not too deep, and a roasting rack (or some kitchen foil), and a small baking tray.

Pre-heat the oven to gas mark 9, 475°F (240°C).

Buy the pork a couple of days before you need to cook it, remove any plastic wrapping, then put the pork on a plate immediately and dry it as thoroughly as possible with absorbent kitchen paper. After that, leave it, uncovered, in the lowest part of the fridge, so that the skin can become as dry as possible before you start the cooking.

While the oven is pre-heating, score the skin of the pork. It will be scored already, but it's always best to add a few more lines. To do this you can use the point of a very sharp paring knife, or Stanley knife, or you can now even buy a special scalpel from a good-quality kitchen shop! What you need to do is score the skin all over into thin strips, bringing the blade of the knife about halfway through the fat beneath the skin.

The golden rule for crunchy crackling is firstly, not to use too deep a roasting tin as this creates too much steam, and secondly, to keep the rind of the pork so it sits above the sides of the tin – this can be achieved by using a roasting rack or, failing that, take a very large piece of foil and crumple it to make yourself a roasting rack to sit the pork on. Then put the onion halves in the tin, as these will caramelise and give a lovely flavour to the gravy. Now take about 1 tablespoon of crushed sea salt crystals and sprinkle them evenly over the skin, pressing them in as much as you can. Place the pork on a high shelf in the oven and roast it for 20 minutes. Turn the heat down to gas mark 5, 375°F (190°C) and cook the pork for a further 2½ hours. There's no need to baste pork, as there is enough fat to keep the meat moist.

About half an hour before the end of the cooking time of the pork, prepare the stuffed apples. First of all, in a small basin mix the sausagemeat, chopped thyme and parsley and add a good seasoning of salt and pepper (if you're using sausages, just slit the skins lengthways and peel them off). Using a potato peeler or an apple corer, remove the core from the apples, then cut out a little more apple with a sharp knife to make the cavity slightly larger. Now divide the sausagemeat mixture into 8. Then roll each portion into a sausage shape and fit that into the cavity of each apple. There will be some at the top that won't go in, so just pat that into a round neat shape. Now make a small incision around the central circumference of the apple. Brush each one with melted butter and insert a little sprig of thyme on top. Place the apples on the baking tray.

The way to tell if the meat is cooked is to insert a skewer in the thickest part and the juices that run out should be absolutely clear without any trace of pinkness. When the pork is cooked, remove it from the oven and pop the apples in to roast for about 25 minutes. Give the pork at least 30 minutes' resting time before carving.

While that is happening, tilt the tin and spoon all the fat off, leaving only the juices. The onion will probably be black and charred, which gives the gravy a lovely rich colour. Leave the onion in, then place the roasting tin over a direct heat, turned to low, sprinkle in the flour and quickly work it into the juices with a wooden spoon. Now turn the heat up to medium and gradually add the cider and the stock, this time using a balloon whisk, until it comes up to simmering point and you have a smooth, rich gravy. Taste and season with salt and pepper, then discard the onion and pour the gravy into a warm serving jug. Serve the pork, carved in slices, giving everyone some crackling and a roasted apple.

Pork Chops Baked with Wild Mushrooms and Crème Fraîche
Serves 6

6 large pork chops

½ oz (10 g) dried porcini mushrooms

7 fl oz (200 ml) crème fraîche

2-3 oz (50-75 g) butter

1 dessertspoon chopped fresh thyme, plus 6 sprigs

12 oz (350 g) dark-gilled, open-cap mushrooms

juice of 1 large lemon

1½ tablespoons plain flour

salt and freshly milled black pepper

You will need a roasting tin, about 10 x 12 inches (25.5 x 30 cm), and a large double sheet of foil.

Pre-heat the oven to gas mark 4, 350°F (180°C).

This is quite simply the best recipe I've ever done for pork chops. Years ago, I had to make do with just cultivated mushrooms and double cream, which always tended to separate in the cooking. Now, with the addition of porcini mushrooms and that heavenly ingredient crème fraîche, the recipe is even more wonderful.

First of all, place the porcini mushrooms in a bowl, pour on enough boiling water just to cover them, then leave them to soak for 20 minutes. Next, place a sheet of foil (large enough to wrap the chops in) in the roasting tin. Now, in a large frying pan, melt 2 oz (50 g) of the butter and fry the chops to a nice, nutty, golden colour on both sides. As you brown them, transfer them on to the foil, then season each one with salt and freshly milled black pepper and sprinkle on the chopped thyme.

Now chop the open-cap mushrooms roughly and fry them in the same pan you browned the meat in, adding a little more butter, if you think it needs it. When the juices start to run, drain the porcini, squeeze out any excess moisture, then chop them small and add them to the fresh mushrooms, along with the lemon juice. Let the lemon juice bubble for about 1 minute, then sprinkle in the flour and stir with a wooden spoon, absolutely ignoring what it looks like, as all will be well in the end!

Now spoon the mixture over the pork chops, then, top each one with a large blob of crème fraîche. Place a sprig of thyme on each, then wrap up loosely in the foil, sealing securely, but leaving some space between the chops and the foil. Finally, bake in the oven for 1 hour exactly. Serve the chops with all the delicious juices poured over and, as this is very rich, you need to keep the vegetables quite simple.

Pork with Apples and Calvados
Serves 2

2 large pork chops

1 large Cox's apple, cored and cut into ½ inch (1 cm) dice with the skin left on

2 tablespoons Calvados

1 tablespoon groundnut or other flavourless oil

½ oz (10 g) butter

1 large shallot, finely chopped

1 dessertspoon caster sugar

7 fl oz (200 ml) dry cider

1½ tablespoons crème fraîche

salt and freshly milled black pepper

You will also need a medium, solid frying pan.

There are some luxuries in the kitchen that really do help to perk up certain dishes, and one of these is a bottle of Calvados because it seems to have within it all the concentrated aroma and flavour of an apple loft. This recipe can be doubled for four people, using a larger pan. It is great served with new potatoes and fine green beans to absorb all that lovely sauce.

First of all, heat half the oil and half the butter in the frying pan over a medium heat. Then add the apple and shallot, together with the sugar, and turn the heat up high. Toss everything around until caramelised and tinged brown at the edges (this will take about 6-8 minutes), then use a draining spoon to transfer them on to a plate to cool.

Next, pat the chops dry with a piece of kitchen paper and season them with salt and pepper. Now add the rest of the oil and butter to the pan and, keeping the heat high, brown the chops for about 5 minutes on each side. After that, heat the Calvados in a small saucepan and, when it is hot, set light to it and pour it carefully over the browned chops (it's a good idea to have a large pan lid handy just in case!).

When the flames have died down, pour the cider into the pan, lower the heat to medium and allow the sauce to bubble and reduce for about 15 minutes or until it has turned syrupy. After that, stir in the crème fraîche and reduce the heat. Return the caramelised apples and shallots to the pan to heat through briefly, then taste to check the seasoning. Serve the chops with the sauce poured over them.

Pork with Pickled Walnut Stuffing
Serves 8

2 large pork fillets (15 oz/425 g each after trimming)

2 oz (50 g) butter, softened

salt and freshly milled black pepper

For the stuffing

4 pickled walnuts in malt vinegar, drained and coarsely chopped

1 oz (25 g) butter

1 medium onion, finely chopped

4 oz (110 g) fresh white breadcrumbs

1 Bramley cooking apple (8 oz/225 g), peeled, cored and diced

zest and juice of ½ lemon

1 large egg, lightly beaten

½ teaspoon dried sage

salt and freshly milled black pepper

For the sauce

1½ tablespoons plain flour

8 fl oz (225 ml) dry cider

8 fl oz (225 ml) good-quality chicken stock

salt and freshly milled black pepper

You will also need a 10 x 14 x 2 inch (25.5 x 35.5 x 5 cm) roasting tin, the base lightly buttered, and some string.

Pre-heat the oven to gas mark 5, 375°F, 190°C.

This might sound unlikely but it's a great combination. The sharpness of the pickled walnuts complements the richness of the pork perfectly.

Start off by cutting one of the pork fillets almost in half lengthways (using a sharp knife) and open the 2 halves out. Now do the same with the other fillet. Next, use a rolling pin to bash the fillets all the way down to flatten them a bit, they need to be about 5-6 inches (13-15 cm) wide, then season them with salt and freshly milled black pepper.

Now prepare the stuffing. Heat 1 oz (25 g) of the butter in a small saucepan, then gently fry the chopped onion for 10 minutes until softened, and add it (and its juices) to a bowl containing the remaining stuffing ingredients: the breadcrumbs, walnuts, apple, lemon zest and juice, egg and sage.

Now mix everything lightly together, taste and season, then pile half of the stuffing along the length of one half of one of the split fillets. Fold the other half of the fillet over the top, then tie with string to keep it in shape. Then do the same with the other fillet and the rest of the stuffing. Next, rub each fillet with 1 oz (25 g) of butter, place them in the roasting tin and bake for about 40-50 minutes, basting now and then.

When the fillets are cooked, remove them to a warmed serving dish and now make the sauce. Place the roasting tin over direct heat and stir in the flour. Mix, then allow this to brown for a couple of minutes before gradually stirring in the cider and stock. Let it bubble for a bit and reduce for 3-4 minutes, then season and strain the sauce and serve immediately with the meat, cut into slices.

Roast Loin of Pork with Honey and Ginger, with a Purée of Apples and Ginger
Serves 6

4 lb (1.8 kg) loin pork, chined (backbone loosened – ask the butcher to do this for you), and with the rind scored

1 teaspoon runny honey

1½ oz (40 g) fresh root ginger

1 teaspoon ground ginger

20 whole cloves

1 medium onion, halved

sea salt and freshly milled black pepper

For the purée

2 medium Bramley cooking apples

1 large Cox's apple

1 rounded dessertspoon freshly grated ginger

1 oz (25 g) butter

1 medium onion, finely chopped

1 oz (25 g) golden caster sugar

3 tablespoons dry cider

salt and freshly milled black pepper

For the gravy

1 rounded tablespoon plain flour

10 fl oz (275 ml) dry cider

about 5 fl oz (150 ml) vegetable stock (or vegetable cooking water)

salt and freshly milled black pepper

In order to ensure you get really crisp crackling, dry the rind thoroughly when you get the pork home, then place the pork, uncovered, in the fridge to allow the rind to dry out.

First of all, you need to insert the cloves and ginger into the pork, so begin by peeling the ginger, then cutting it into little strips vaguely half the length of matchsticks. Then take your smallest, sharpest-pointed knife and begin to make slits in between the pork rind and right down into the flesh, then push a piece of ginger into each slit as you make it. When half the ginger has been inserted, turn the joint upside down and do the same on the other side, sliding the knife in between the bones and, again, trying to get the ginger well into the flesh of the pork. After that, insert the cloves here and there in both sides, pushing these well into the same little slits. Just before cooking the pork, sprinkle the rind with salt and black pepper, being quite generous and pressing it well in all over. Put the onion halves in the tin, as these will caramelise and give a lovely flavour to the gravy. Now put the pork on a roasting rack in the tin or, failing that, take a very large piece of foil and crumple it to make yourself a roasting rack and sit the pork on top of that. Then, place the pork on a high shelf in the oven. Give it 20 minutes' initial cooking time, then turn the heat down to gas mark 5, 375°F (190°C) and give the pork another 2 hours' cooking. Don't baste it at all, just leave the rind to get really blistered and crisp.

About 20 minutes before the end of the pork's cooking time, make the purée of apples and ginger. Start by melting the butter in a medium saucepan over a gentle heat and soften the onion in it for about 5 minutes. Meanwhile, peel, core and thinly slice the apples and, when the onion is soft, add them to the pan, followed by all the rest of the ingredients. Season, then, keeping the heat low, cover with a lid and cook everything very gently for about 20 minutes, stirring now and then. When the apples are soft and fluffy, beat them with an electric hand whisk or a balloon whisk until they form a soft, smooth purée. Pour the purée into a warm serving bowl and keep warm till you're ready to serve the pork. Then, 5 minutes before the cooking time for the pork is up, increase the oven temperature to gas mark 7, 425°F (220°C). Mix together the honey and ground

You will also need a solid roasting tin, approximately 10 x 12 inches (25.5 x 30 cm) but not too deep, and a roasting rack or some kitchen foil.

Pre-heat the oven to gas mark 9, 475°F (240°C).

ginger, then remove the pork from the oven and quickly paint this mixture all over the rind with a brush. Then back it goes into the oven for a further 5 minutes' cooking time – please use a timer, as at this temperature it can burn if you forget! After that, remove the pork from the oven, transfer it to a carving board and let it relax in a warm place for 30 minutes before carving.

Make the gravy by spooning the excess fat from the roasting tin, leaving about 1½ tablespoons of it behind. Then place the tin over direct heat and sprinkle in the flour, stirring vigorously with a wooden spoon, scraping the base and sides of the tin to remove all the crusty bits. When it's really smooth, begin to add the cider a little at a time, switching to a balloon whisk to whisk everything smoothly. There won't be enough liquid now, so finish it off using some of the vegetable stock, adding as much as you need to make the consistency you want. Let it bubble for a minute, taste to check the seasoning, and pour it into a warm serving jug. To carve, simply slide the knife all the way along the central bone of the pork to remove it. Now remove the rib bones, which will come away in one piece. The pork will then be ready to carve in even slices.

Pork Chops with a Confit of Prunes, Apples and Shallots
Serves 4

4 large pork chops

1 heaped tablespoon flour, seasoned with salt and freshly milled black pepper

1 tablespoon groundnut or other flavourless oil

½ oz (10 g) butter

For the confit

5 oz (150 g) pitted Agen prunes

1 good-sized Granny Smith apple

4 large shallots, each cut into 6 wedges through the root

10 fl oz (275 ml) strong dry cider

2 fl oz (55 ml) cider vinegar

1 tablespoon dark soft brown sugar

2 good pinches of ground cloves

⅛ teaspoon ground mace

For the cider glaze

8 fl oz (225 ml) strong, dry cider

You will also need a solid frying pan with a diameter of 10 inches (25.5 cm).

This is a great recipe. The confit goes equally well with roast pork, and is brilliant served with a rough, pork-based pâté (see page 120).

You can make the confit at any time – the day before, even. All you do is cut the apple into quarters, remove the core, then cut the quarters into ½ inch (1 cm) slices, leaving the skin on. Then just place all the ingredients together in a medium saucepan, bring everything up to a gentle simmer, then let it cook as gently as possible, without a lid, for 45 minutes to an hour – you'll need to stir it from time to time – until all the liquid has reduced to a lovely sticky glaze.

When you're ready to cook the pork chops, dip them lightly in the seasoned flour, shaking off any surplus. Now heat the oil in the frying pan and, when it's really hot, add the butter. As soon as it foams, add the chops and brown them on both sides, keeping the heat fairly high. Then lower the heat and continue to cook the chops gently for about 25 minutes in total, turning them once.

Meanwhile, warm the confit, either in a saucepan, or in a dish covered with foil in a low oven, while you warm the plates; the confit shouldn't be hot – just warm. After that, increase the heat under the frying pan, then pour in the cider for the glaze and let it bubble briskly and reduce to half its original volume, which should take about 5 minutes. Serve the chops on the warmed plates, with the cider glaze spooned over and some confit on the side.

Stuffed Pork Tenderloin with Fresh Herbs
Serves 4

1 large pork fillet (about 1 lb/450 g)

4 rashers unsmoked streaky bacon, derinded

¾ oz (20 g) softened butter

salt and freshly milled black pepper

For the stuffing

1 oz (25 g) butter

1 medium onion, finely chopped

1 dessertspoon chopped fresh thyme

1 dessertspoon chopped fresh sage

3 oz (75 g) small open-cap mushrooms, finely chopped

4 oz (110 g) fresh white breadcrumbs

4 tablespoons chopped fresh parsley

the grated zest of a lemon

2 teaspoons lemon juice

1 large egg lightly beaten with 2 tablespoons double cream

salt and freshly milled black pepper

For the gravy

1 tablespoon plain flour

10 fl oz (275 ml) dry white wine

You will also need a 9 x 11 x 2 inch (23 x 28 x 5 cm) roasting tin, buttered, and some string.

Pre-heat the oven to gas mark 4, 350°F, 180°C.

This is a good recipe for a dinner party as it's easy to carve and serve. To serve eight, just double the ingredients using two fillets.

Do not trim the fat from the tenderloin as this will help to keep it moist. Slice it in half lengthways, batter the 2 halves with a rolling pin to flatten and widen them slightly, then season with salt and freshly milled pepper.

Next, to prepare the stuffing, melt the butter in a medium frying pan and fry the onion gently over a medium heat for 10 minutes or until softened, then stir in the herbs and mushrooms and raise the heat slightly. Cook for 3 or 4 minutes, then transfer the contents of the pan to a bowl and add the remaining stuffing ingredients. Fork the mixture together lightly, taste and season. Now pat the stuffing on to one half of the tenderloin, and replace the other half on top. Smear the fillet with the softened butter and season with freshly milled pepper.

Then lay the bacon on top of the fillet to cover it. Tie the fillet round with string at about 2 inch (5 cm) intervals to hold the whole thing together, slip a long palette knife under its length and transfer to the buttered roasting tin. Bake in the top half of the oven for 1 hour. Then transfer the fillet to a dish to keep warm and now make the gravy. Place the tin over direct heat and sprinkle in the flour to soak up the juices, stirring vigorously with a wooden spoon. Then, when it's smooth, gradually add the wine, switching to a balloon whisk to whisk everything together and then let the gravy bubble till syrupy. Serve the pork, cut into thick slices, with the gravy poured over, and perhaps a garnish of fried apple rings (see page 8).

Smoked Loin of Pork with Citrus, Rum and Raisin Sauce
Serves 6

2 lb 8 oz (1.15 kg) smoked, cured pork loin joint

For the sauce

1 large juicy orange

1 lime

3 fl oz (75 ml) dark rum

3 oz (75 g) raisins

4 oz (110 g) dark soft brown sugar

1 slightly rounded teaspoon arrowroot

You will also need a small, solid, shallow roasting tin.

This is a very easy joint to carve, and serving it with a citrus, rum and raisin sauce is a heavenly combination. If possible, make this sweet-sharp sauce the day before you need it, so the raisins have plenty of time to absorb all the flavours and become nice and plump.

Begin by making the sauce. All you do is remove the outer zest from the orange using a potato peeler so that you don't get any of the pith. Then pile the little strips on top of one another and, using a very sharp knife, cut them into really thin needle-sized strips. If you've got the orange peel piled up, and your knife is sharp, this is a lot easier than it sounds. Next, remove the zest from the lime, this time using a fine grater, and squeeze the juice from the lime and the orange.

Place all the sauce ingredients, except the arrowroot, into a small saucepan. Now whisk the arrowroot into the mixture and place the pan on to a gentle heat, whisking all the time until it starts to simmer. As soon as this happens, the sauce will change from opaque to clear, so then remove it from the heat and when it is cool enough, pour it into a serving dish, cover with clingfilm and chill until needed.

When you are ready to cook the pork, pre-heat the oven to gas mark 4, 350°F (180°C) and cook the joint in the roasting tin for 1 hour 50 minutes. Serve the pork, carved in slices, with some sauce spooned over.

Roast Tenderloin of Pork with Mustard and Crème Fraîche Sauce
Serves 4

2 thick pork fillets (12 oz/350 g each after trimming)

1 large egg

1 heaped dessertspoon wholegrain mustard

1 heaped dessertspoon Dijon mustard

2 cloves garlic, peeled

½ oz (10 g) fresh curly parsley

4 heaped tablespoons fresh white breadcrumbs

salt and freshly milled black pepper

For the sauce

1 dessertspoon each wholegrain mustard and Dijon mustard

1 tablespoon crème fraîche

½ oz (10 g) butter

1 medium onion, finely chopped

11 fl oz (310 ml) dry white wine

You will also need a medium baking tray (it needs to be a little longer than the pork fillets), greased.

Pre-heat the oven to gas mark 5, 375°F (190°C).

This is what we all need when time is short – a very easy, speedy recipe that is quick to make but tastes exceptionally good.

First of all, trim the excess fat and sinew from the pork fillets. Then, in a small bowl, beat the egg together with the 2 mustards and pour it into an oblong dish, which is at least 1 inch (2.5 cm) deep and as long as the pork fillets. Next, chop the garlic and parsley (in a mini-chopper or processor, if you have one), add the breadcrumbs and a seasoning of salt and pepper, whiz for a couple of seconds, then spread them out on to another oblong dish (the same size as above).

Now roll the pork fillets in the egg mixture first, until they are very well coated. Then lift them out of the egg mixture, letting the excess egg drip back into the dish, and lay them in the crumb mixture. Turn the fillets over in the crumbs until they are evenly coated and there are almost no loose crumbs left in the dish.

After that, transfer them to the greased baking tray and roast the fillets in the pre-heated oven for 30 minutes. This will give you pork that is still slightly pink in the middle. If you prefer it more well done, cook it for a further 10 minutes. (If you are preparing the pork a couple of hours in advance, just cover it with clingfilm and keep it in the fridge till needed but allow it to come back to room temperature before cooking.)

Meanwhile, for the sauce, heat the butter in a small saucepan and cook the onion in it on a medium heat for about 10 minutes until softened and golden brown. Then add the white wine, turn up the heat and boil for 10 minutes to reduce slightly, before adding the crème fraîche and mustards, then simmer gently for a further 10 minutes. When the pork is cooked, let it rest in a warm place for about 10 minutes before carving into slices and serving with the sauce.

Pork Florentine
Serves 2-3

1 large pork fillet (14 oz/400 g after trimming)

1 lb 8 oz (700 g) young leaf spinach

freshly grated nutmeg

½ oz (10 g) butter

2 tablespoons groundnut or other flavourless oil

1 medium onion, finely chopped

salt and freshly milled black pepper

For the sauce

15 fl oz (425 ml) dry white wine

1 oz (25 g) butter

½ oz (10 g) plain flour

5 fl oz (150 ml) milk

1½ oz (40 g) Cheshire cheese, grated

3½ fl oz (100 ml) single cream

salt and freshly milled black pepper

For the topping

2 tablespoons white breadcrumbs

1 tablespoon freshly grated Parmesan

You will also need an ovenproof dish, 6 x 10 x 1½ inches (15 x 25.5 x 4 cm), buttered.

There are many recipes around the world that combine pork and cheese and this one is an absolute winner. With the spinach all you need are some small steamed new potatoes for a complete meal.

First, cut the fillet into slices about ¼ inch (5 mm) thick, then cut each slice into chip-like strips. Pre-heat the oven to a low setting and put the dish in to heat at the same time. Meanwhile, cook the spinach by putting it in a large saucepan with a lid on, then place it over a medium heat. Just let it collapse down into its own juices, timing it for 2-3 minutes and turning it over halfway through. Drain the spinach in a colander, pressing it with a saucer to extract every last bit of juice, then arrange it in the bottom of the dish. Season with salt, pepper and a grating of nutmeg, then cover and keep warm in the oven.

Next, heat the ½ oz (10 g) of butter and 1 tablespoon of the oil in a frying pan and fry the onion over a medium heat for 10 minutes or till softened and golden, then sprinkle this over the spinach. Now heat the rest of the oil and fry the pork strips over a fairly high heat till brown in 3 separate batches for 2 minutes on each side. Then use a draining spoon to transfer the pork to the dish, scattering it on top of the spinach and onion, cover and keep warm in the oven.

Next, pour the wine into the frying pan and let it bubble away over a highish heat while you scrape any meat sediments from the base and sides, then leave it to reduce down to about 2 tablespoons. Meanwhile, to make the sauce heat the butter in a separate pan, stir in the flour and, over a medium heat and using a small pointed wooden spoon, stir quite vigorously to make a smooth, glossy paste. Now begin to add the milk and reduced wine a little at a time. Then, when about half the milk and wine are in, switch to a balloon whisk and start adding larger amounts, whisking briskly. Now turn the heat down to its lowest setting and let the sauce cook for 2 minutes, whisking from time to time. Remove the dish from the oven and pre-heat the grill to its highest setting.

Stir the cheese and cream into the sauce, taste and season and then pour it over the pork strips. Finally, sprinkle with the breadcrumbs and Parmesan, and brown briefly under a high grill until hot and bubbling, and serve at once.

Pork Chops with Sage and Apples
Serves 4

4 large, lean pork chops

3 dessertspoons very finely chopped fresh sage

2 Cox's apples, cored and sliced into rings but with skins left on

4-6 oz (110-175 g) white breadcrumbs made from day-old bread

1 large egg

about 3 tablespoons groundnut or other flavourless oil

about 2 oz (50 g) butter

1 medium onion, sliced into rings

salt and freshly milled black pepper

You will also need a large, solid frying pan with a diameter of 10 inches (25.5 cm), and a medium, solid frying pan.

This is an excellent recipe and a very old favourite of mine. It is blissfully simple but never disappoints.

First of all, mix the sage and breadcrumbs together and season well with salt and freshly milled black pepper. Then beat the egg and dip the pork chops first in the egg, then into the breadcrumb and sage mixture, pressing firmly all round so that the chops get a really good, even coating.

Now heat 2 tablespoons of the oil and 1 oz (25 g) of butter together in the large frying pan and, first of all, brown the chops quickly on both sides with the fat fairly hot, then lower the heat and let them gently cook through (it will take around 25-30 minutes depending on the thickness of the chops).

While that's happening, melt the rest of the butter and oil in the other frying pan and fry the apple and onion rings, this will take about 10 minutes. Drain everything on crumpled baking parchment or greaseproof paper before serving.

Fast Roast Pork with Rosemary and Caramelised Apples
Serves 6

2 thick pork fillets
(12 oz/350 g each after trimming)

1 rounded tablespoon fresh
rosemary leaves

3 Granny Smith apples,
skins left on, cored and cut
into 6 wedges each

2 cloves garlic, cut into thin slices

1½ oz (40 g) butter

1½ tablespoons cider vinegar

1 small onion, finely chopped

1 tablespoon demerara sugar

8 fl oz (225 ml) strong dry cider

2 heaped tablespoons half-fat
crème fraîche

salt and freshly milled
black pepper

You will also need a flameproof
baking tray, 11 x 16 inches
(28 x 40 cm), lightly buttered.

Pre-heat the oven to gas mark 8,
450°F (230°C).

It's hard to believe that you can serve a roast for six people in about 40 minutes flat from start to finish, but you can, and here it is. It's also outstandingly good, dead simple, can be prepared in advance and, once tried, I'm sure you'll want to make it again and again.

First of all, using a small, sharp knife, make little slits all over the pork and push the slivers of garlic into them, turning each fillet over so the garlic is in on both sides. Next, place the rosemary leaves in a mortar and bruise them with a pestle to release their fragrant oil, then chop them very finely.

Now melt the butter and combine it with the cider vinegar, then brush the meat with some of this mixture, sprinkle with half the rosemary and season with salt and pepper. Scatter the onion over the buttered baking tray and place the pork on top. All this can be prepared in advance, then covered with clingfilm.

When you want to cook the roast, prepare the apples by tossing them with the remaining cider vinegar and butter mixture, then arrange them all around the pork on the baking tray and sprinkle with the sugar and the rest of the rosemary. Place the baking tray in the oven on a high shelf and roast for 25-30 minutes (this will depend on the thickness of the pork), or until the pork is cooked through.

After that, remove the baking tray from the oven and transfer the pork and apples to a hot serving dish, cover with foil and keep warm. Meanwhile, pour a little of the cider on to the tray, over the heat, to loosen the onions and juices from it, then pour this into a saucepan over a medium heat, add the rest of the cider and let it bubble and reduce by about a third – this will take about 5 minutes. Then whisk in the crème fraîche, let it bubble a bit more and add some seasoning.

After the pork has rested for about 10 minutes, transfer it to a board and carve it into thick slices, then return them to the serving dish to rejoin the apples. Pour the sauce over and serve as soon as possible. Roast potatoes are particularly good with this.

Classic Roast Leg of Pork with Crackling, Sage and Onion Stuffing and Eliza Acton's Oven-baked Apple Sauce
Serves 8

a 5 lb (2.25 kg) piece of boneless leg of pork, with the rind scored

1 small onion

1 tablespoon sea salt

1 tablespoon plain flour

10 fl oz (275 ml) dry white wine

10 fl oz (275 ml) vegetable stock (or vegetable cooking water)

salt and freshly milled black pepper

For the sage and onion stuffing

1 lb (450 g) good-quality pork sausagemeat or sausages

½ oz (10 g) chopped fresh sage

1 small onion, very finely chopped

1½ oz (40 g) white breadcrumbs, made from day-old bread

salt and freshly milled black pepper

For Eliza Acton's oven-baked apple sauce

1 lb 8 oz (700 g) Bramley cooking apples, peeled, quartered and cored

1 oz (25 g) golden caster sugar

a small knob of butter

You will also need a solid roasting tin, approximately 10 x 12 inches (25.5 x 30 cm), and a baking dish, 6 x 10 x 2 inches (15 x 25.5 x 5 cm), lightly buttered.

Pre-heat the oven to gas mark 4, 350°F (180°C).

I would not have believed apple sauce could be so much improved by following Eliza Acton's recipe from her book published in 1845. I sometimes leave the peel on the apples but I think that is a personal choice.

To make the apple sauce, put the apples into a pudding basin or small casserole with the sugar and sprinkle a tablespoon of water over them. Then, put a lid on (I use a saucepan lid with a pudding basin) and bake in the oven for about 35 minutes, or until the apples are soft and reduced to a pulp. Next, add the butter and beat the apples with a wooden spoon until smooth, then transfer to a serving dish.

Meanwhile, score the skin of the pork. It will be scored already, but it's always best to add a few more lines. To do this you can use the point of a very sharp paring knife, a Stanley knife, or a special scalpel from a good-quality kitchen shop. What you need to do is score the skin all over into thin strips, bringing the blade of the knife about halfway through the fat beneath the skin. When the apple sauce is ready, increase the oven temperature to gas mark 9, 475°F (240°C).

Now place the pork in the roasting tin, skin side up, halve the onion and wedge the 2 pieces in slightly underneath the meat. Now take a tablespoon of crushed sea salt crystals and sprinkle it evenly over the skin, pressing it in as much as you can. Place the pork on a high shelf in the oven and roast it for 20 minutes. Turn the heat down to gas mark 5, 375°F (190°C) and cook the pork for a further 2½ hours. There's no need to baste pork as there is enough fat to keep the meat moist.

For the stuffing, combine the breadcrumbs with the sage and onion in a mixing bowl, then stir in 1 tablespoon of boiling water and mix thoroughly together. Next, work the sausagemeat into this mixture and season generously with salt and freshly milled black pepper (if you're using sausages, just slit the skins lengthways and peel them off). Transfer the stuffing to the baking dish and put it in the oven for the last 30 minutes of the pork's cooking time.

The way to tell if the pork is cooked is to insert a skewer into the thickest part and the juices that run out should be absolutely clear without any trace of pinkness. When the pork is cooked, remove it from the oven and give it at least 30 minutes' resting time before carving.

While that is happening, tilt the tin and spoon all the fat off, leaving only the juices. The onion will probably be black and charred, which gives the gravy a lovely rich colour. Leave the onion in, then place the roasting tin over a direct heat, turned to low, sprinkle in the flour and quickly work it into the juices with a wooden spoon. Now turn the heat up to medium and gradually add the wine and the stock, this time using a balloon whisk, until it comes up to simmering point and you have a smooth, rich gravy. Taste and season with salt and pepper, then discard the onion and pour the gravy into a warm serving jug. Serve the pork carved in slices, giving everyone some crackling and stuffing, and hand the apple sauce around separately.

Pork Stroganoff with Three Mustards
Serves 2

1 thick pork fillet
(12 oz/350 g after trimming)

1 teaspoon English mustard
powder

1 heaped teaspoon wholegrain
mustard

1 heaped teaspoon Dijon mustard

4 oz (110 g) small open-cap
mushrooms

7 fl oz (200 ml) crème fraîche

1 dessertspoon groundnut or other
flavourless oil

½ oz (10 g) butter

1 small onion, halved and thinly
sliced

3 fl oz (75 ml) dry white wine

salt and freshly milled
black pepper

You will also need a 9 inch (23 cm)
solid frying pan.

This is what I'd call a five-star supper dish for two people, with the added bonus that it only takes about 20 minutes to prepare from start to finish. Serve it with plain boiled basmati rice and a salad of tossed green leaves.

First of all, prepare the pork by trimming it and cutting it into strips 3 inches (7.5 cm) long and ¼ inch (5 mm) wide. Then prepare the mushrooms by slicing them through the stalk into thin slices.

Now, in a small bowl, mix together the three mustards with the crème fraîche and, when you're ready to cook the pork, take the frying pan and heat the oil and butter together over a medium heat. Add the onion slices and fry them gently for about 2-3 minutes until they're soft.

Using a draining spoon, remove the onions to a plate, turn the heat up under the pan to its highest setting and, when it's smoking hot, add the strips of pork and fry them quickly, keeping them on the move all the time so they cook evenly, without burning. Then add the mushrooms and toss these around to cook very briefly until their juices start to run. After that, return the onion slices to the pan and stir them in. Season well with salt and pepper, then add the wine and let it bubble and reduce slightly before adding the mustard and crème fraîche mixture. Now stir the whole lot together and let the sauce bubble and reduce to half its original volume. Serve immediately, spooned over rice.

Casseroles Braising

Poor Man's Cassoulet
Serves 4-6

12 fat, good-quality pork sausages with high meat content

12 oz (350 g) dried cannellini beans

1 dessertspoon olive oil

9 oz (250 g) cubetti di pancetta, or you can use diced bacon

3 medium onions, thinly sliced

3 fat cloves garlic, finely chopped

1 tablespoon fresh thyme leaves, plus a few sprigs

2 bay leaves

2 tablespoons tomato purée

4 oz (110 g) white breadcrumbs made from day-old bread

salt and freshly milled black pepper

You will also need a 6 pint (3.5 litre), lidded, flameproof casserole.

Pre-heat the oven to gas mark 1, 275°F (140°C).

This is a modern version of an original recipe that appeared in my book, *Frugal Food*, and, I suppose, while it lacks sophisticated ingredients like preserved goose, it's still very much on the theme of the original. This is very rich and hefty, so a green salad is really all it needs to go with it.

Ideally, you need to start the cassoulet the night before you want to make it by rinsing the dried cannellini beans in a sieve under cold water, and then placing them in a bowl with 3 pints (1.75 litres) of cold water to soak overnight. If you are short of time, put the beans in a saucepan with the same amount of cold water, bring them up to the boil and give them about 10 minutes' cooking before turning the heat off and leaving them to soak for 2 hours. Either way, after soaking, drain the beans in a colander.

Then, in the flameproof casserole, heat the oil over a medium heat and brown the sausages, turning them occasionally because they need to be a nice golden brown colour on all sides – this will take 7-8 minutes. After that, remove them to a plate, then add the pancetta to the casserole, turning the heat up and tossing it around for 5 minutes, until it's golden at the edges. Now, using a slotted spoon, transfer the pancetta to join the sausages. Turn the heat down to medium, then in the juices left in the casserole, soften the onions for 10 minutes, stirring from time to time.

After that, toss in the garlic and cook for another minute, then transfer the onion and garlic to another plate. Next, put a third of the beans into the casserole, followed by half the onions, sprinkle with a third of the fresh thyme leaves and season well with salt and pepper, then add half the sausages and pancetta, followed by a third more of the beans, thyme and seasoning, then the remaining sausages, pancetta and onions and finally, the rest of the beans and thyme leaves, pushing the sprigs of thyme and bay leaves in among everything. Now measure 1½ pints (850 ml) of boiling water, whisk in the tomato purée and pour this over the beans, cover with a lid, and bake on the oven's centre shelf for 2 hours. Then take the lid off, sprinkle the breadcrumbs all over the top and bake (without a lid) for a further hour until the beans are completely cooked through.

Oriental Pork Casserole with Stir-fried Green Vegetables
Serves 4-6

2 lb (900 g) shoulder of pork, chopped into 1 inch (2.5 cm) cubes

4 fl oz (120 ml) Japanese soy sauce

1 rounded tablespoon freshly grated peeled root ginger

1 dessertspoon molasses sugar

1 small onion, finely chopped

2 cloves garlic, crushed

2 medium red chillies, deseeded and finely chopped

4 fl oz (120 ml) Shaosing brown rice wine or dry sherry

2 x 3 inch (7.5 cm) cinnamon sticks

2 whole star anise

For the stir-fried green vegetables

4 oz (110 g) cauliflower

6 oz (175 g) broccoli

2 medium leeks

4 spring onions

a 2 inch (5 cm) piece root ginger, peeled

10 oz (275 g) small pak choi

2 tablespoons groundnut or other flavourless oil

2 cloves garlic, thinly sliced

3 tablespoons Japanese soy sauce

3 fl oz (75 ml) Shaosing brown rice wine or dry sherry

1 dessertspoon caster sugar

To garnish

2 spring onions

½ medium red chilli, deseeded

You will also need a 4 pint (2.25 litre) lidded, flameproof casserole.

This is quite an exotic recipe, a wonderful combination of flavours that develop and permeate the pork as it cooks very slowly. The surprising thing is the casserole takes only 6 minutes or so to prepare from start to finish. Serve it with Thai fragrant rice. If you like, spinach leaves can be used instead of pak choi.

All you need to do is arrange the pork in a single layer in the base of the casserole, then simply mix all the other ingredients (except the cinnamon and star anise) together, give them a good whisk and pour over the pork. Now tuck in the cinnamon sticks and star anise, place the casserole on the hob and bring everything up to a very gentle simmer. Put the lid on and simmer over the gentlest possible heat for 45 minutes. At that point turn the pieces of pork over, replace the lid and simmer for 45 minutes more.

For the stir-fry, first prepare the vegetables: the cauliflower should be separated out and cut into tiny florets, and the same with the broccoli. Wash and trim the leeks, then halve and thinly slice them, while the spring onions should be sliced into matchsticks, as should the ginger. Finally, cut each head of pak choi into 6 wedges through the root.

When you're ready to cook, heat the oil over a high heat in a wok. Add the ginger and garlic and fry for 10 seconds, then add the cauliflower and broccoli and stir-fry for 1 minute. Next, add the leeks and stir-fry for another minute. Add the spring onions and pak choi, toss everything together, then add the soy sauce and brown rice wine, plus 3 fl oz (75 ml) water, and the sugar. Reduce the heat to medium, put a lid on and cook for 4 minutes, stirring occasionally. For the garnish, cut the spring onions into fine shreds, 1 inch (2.5 cm) long and cut the chilli into fine shreds, too. Serve the pork and stir-fried greens with the spring onions and chilli sprinkled over each portion, remembering to remove the cinnamon sticks and star anise first.

Braised Pork with Apples and Cider
Serves 4

4 thick, lean belly pork strips or spare rib chops (1 lb 8 oz/700 g), trimmed

1 large Bramley apple, peeled, cored and sliced

5 fl oz (150 ml) dry cider

1 tablespoon olive oil

6 rashers unsmoked streaky bacon, derinded

6 juniper berries, crushed with the back of a spoon

2 cloves garlic, finely chopped

2 medium onions, chopped small

1 lb 8 oz (700 g) Desirée or King Edward potatoes, peeled and thickly sliced (¼ inch/5 mm slices)

1 oz (25 g) butter

salt and freshly milled black pepper

You will also need a large frying pan, a wide, shallow, 4 pint (2.25 litre), lidded casserole, and some foil.

Pre-heat the oven to gas mark 1, 275°F (140°C).

This is a hearty winter dish that can be left on its own for 3 hours if you plan to be out. You could also leave some red cabbage to braise in the oven with it and return to a complete meal.

If the pork is very fatty, trim away the excess fat, then heat the oil in the frying pan and brown the pork on both sides, then transfer it to the casserole. Next, in the same pan, fry the bacon rashers a little until the fat starts to run. Then, using a draining spoon, place the bacon on top of the pork and season, but be careful with the salt as there'll be some in the bacon.

Now sprinkle over the juniper berries and garlic, then spread the slices of apple and the chopped onion on top. Add the cider and cover with a layer of overlapping potatoes. Finally, put a few dabs of butter on top, cover the dish first with foil, and then with a close-fitting lid. Transfer to the oven and cook for 3 hours. Towards the end of the cooking time, pre-heat the grill to its highest setting. When the oven time is completed, place the dish, uncovered, under the grill so the potatoes become brown and crispy.

Braised Pork with Boston Baked Beans
Serves 4-6

12 oz (350 g) streaky belly of pork, in one piece with rind on

1 lb (450 g) dried white haricot beans

1 teaspoon English mustard powder

2 tablespoons dark soft brown sugar

2 tablespoons tomato purée

2 cloves garlic, crushed

4 tablespoons ready-made barbecue sauce

2 tablespoons molasses or black treacle

1 medium onion, sliced

1 bay leaf

salt and freshly milled black pepper

You will also need a deep, 6 pint (3.5 litre) casserole with a tight-fitting lid.

This is how baked beans should be – the real American sort and not a bit like the ones that come in tins, although I've added a little cheat here to get extra smokey flavour. Serve with sausages or Devilled Spare Ribs (see page 115) and crisp, crunchy jacket potatoes.

Ideally, you need to start this the night before you want to make it by rinsing the haricot beans in a sieve under cold water, and then placing them in a large bowl with 3 pints (1.75 litres) of cold water to soak overnight. If you are short of time, put the beans in a large saucepan with the same amount of cold water, bring them up to the boil and give them about 10 minutes' cooking before turning the heat off and leaving them to soak for 2 hours.

After soaking, drain the beans in a colander, reserving the liquor, then measure out 1 pint (570 ml) of the liquor and throw away the rest. Transfer the beans to the casserole and pre-heat the oven to gas mark $\frac{1}{2}$, 250°F (120°C). At this stage, blend the mustard powder with a little of the measured bean liquor, followed by the sugar, tomato purée, crushed garlic, barbecue sauce and molasses or black treacle. Pour this mixture over the beans, along with the rest of the pint (570 ml) of liquid, some salt and freshly milled black pepper, the sliced onion and bay leaf and give everything a good stir.

Now cut slashes across the pork (approximately $\frac{1}{2}$ inch/1 cm apart) and bury the meat in the beans until only the rind is showing. Then cover the casserole and bake slowly in the centre of the oven for $6\frac{1}{2}$ hours, taking the lid off for the last hour. When the beans are tender, remove the piece of belly pork and take off the rind. It should come away very easily. Finally, using two forks, shred the meat and stir it back into the beans. Serve piping hot.

Note If you do not have a gas mark $\frac{1}{2}$ setting on your gas oven, buy an oven thermometer and test your oven before you start cooking. You'll need to move the dial to different positions between the point where the gas comes on and mark 1. Try halfway, then use the thermometer to see what temperature your oven gives.

Cider-braised Pork with Cream and Mushrooms
Serves 4

12 fl oz (340 ml) dry cider

4 large, thick pork chops

2 tablespoons double cream

8 oz (225 g) small chestnut mushrooms, sliced

2 oz (50 g) butter

1 tablespoon groundnut or other flavourless oil

1 large onion, chopped small

2 cloves of garlic, crushed

1 teaspoon chopped fresh rosemary

1 teaspoon chopped fresh thyme

salt and freshly milled black pepper

You will also need a large, 10 inch (25.5 cm), deep-sided frying pan with a tight-fitting lid.

This recipe was served to me at The Aspall Cyder House in Suffolk, near where I live, about 25 years ago. They gave me this recipe and I'm still making it! For a special occasion, ½ oz (10 g) of dried porcini mushrooms (soaked and roughly chopped) along with the fresh will be a lovely addition.

Begin by seasoning the pork chops with salt and pepper, then heat the butter and oil in the frying pan till foaming and sizzling, and brown the chops for a couple of minutes on both sides so they are a nice golden colour. Then, using a draining spoon, remove them to a plate and keep on one side.

Now add the onion, garlic and mushrooms to the juices left in the pan and cook these together for about 5 minutes, then move them over to one side of the pan and return the chops. Sprinkle them with the herbs, then spoon the mushroom and onion mixture over the top.

Pour in the cider, then turn the heat down to the lowest possible simmer. Cover and simmer gently for 20 minutes. After that, remove the chops, mushrooms and onions to a plate and keep warm in a low oven. Then turn the heat up under the pan and simmer the sauce briskly (with the lid off) for 8 minutes. Now stir in the cream, let it bubble and reduce very slightly, and taste to check the seasoning. Then serve the chops with the sauce poured over.

Marinated Pork with Coriander
Serves 2-3

1 thick pork fillet (12 oz/350 g after trimming), cut into bite-sized cubes

2 heaped teaspoons coriander seeds, crushed

4 tablespoons olive oil

juice of 1 lemon

10 fl oz (275 ml) dry white wine or dry cider

1 fat clove garlic, crushed

salt and freshly milled black pepper

You will also need a large frying pan.

The Greeks call this traditional dish *afelia*. If you have time to leave the meat to steep overnight and for the flavours to develop, so much the better.

Place the pieces of pork in a shallow dish and season them with salt and freshly milled black pepper. Now pour 3 tablespoons of the oil over the meat, followed by the juice of the lemon and 2 tablespoons of the white wine (or cider). Then sprinkle in the crushed coriander seeds and the garlic, and mix everything together. Cover the dish with a cloth and leave it all to marinate overnight – or as long as possible – stirring now and then.

To cook the pork, melt the remaining tablespoon of oil in the frying pan and, when it's fairly hot, add the cubes of pork and cook them over a medium heat, turning them and keeping them on the move. When they have browned a little, pour in the rest of the white wine (or cider), let it bubble and reduce to a syrupy consistency. The pork will take approximately 10-15 minutes to cook altogether. Serve with rice and a salad.

Pork in Cider Vinegar Sauce
Serves 4

2 lb (900 g) pork shoulder, trimmed and cut into 1 inch (2.5 cm) cubes

1 pint (570 ml) medium sweet cider

5 fl oz (150 ml) good-quality cider vinegar

½ oz (10 g) butter

2 tablespoons groundnut or other flavourless oil

12 shallots

4 fresh thyme sprigs

2 bay leaves

1½ tablespoons crème fraîche

salt and freshly milled black pepper

You will also need a wide, shallow, flameproof casserole, with a capacity of 4 pints (2.25 litres).

Pre-heat the oven to gas mark 3, 325°F (170°C).

This recipe has an autumnal ring to it and is, for me, the first casserole of the winter months. Pork shoulder is an excellent cut for braising and this recipe is superb for serving to friends and family because it just cooks away all by itself until you're ready to serve it. I also think it tastes even better the next day so, if you make it that far ahead, don't add the crème fraîche until it's re-heated. The re-heating will take about 25 minutes in a casserole over gentle direct heat. Note here, though, that it's important to use a good-quality cider vinegar. If you don't have a wide, shallow casserole, use an ovenproof dish (same size) but pre-heat it first in the oven. Make sure everything reaches simmering point in the frying pan before you pour it into the dish, then finish the sauce in a saucepan.

First, place the casserole over a fairly high heat and add half the butter and 1 tablespoon of oil. Meanwhile, dry the pieces of meat with kitchen paper, then brown them, a few at a time, in the hot fat, transferring them to a plate as they brown.

After that, add the rest of the butter and oil and, when that's very hot, add the shallots to the casserole and carefully brown these on all sides to a nice, glossy, caramel colour. Now pour the cider and cider vinegar into the casserole, stir well, scraping the base and sides, then return the meat to the casserole, add the thyme and the bay leaves and season well.

As soon as it's all come to simmering point, transfer the casserole, without a lid, to the oven for about 1 hour 15 minutes, or until all the liquid is reduced and the meat is tender. Now remove the meat and shallots to a warm serving dish, discarding the herbs, then place the casserole back over direct heat. Bring it up to the boil and reduce the liquid to about half its original volume. Finally, whisk in the crème fraîche, taste to check the seasoning, then pour the sauce over the meat and serve.

Belly Pork Strips in Barbecue Sauce
Serves 4

3 lb (1.35 kg) belly pork, trimmed and cut into 8 thick strips (trimmed weight 2 lb 8 oz/1.15 kg)

1-2 tablespoons olive oil

1 medium onion, chopped small

freshly milled black pepper

For the sauce

5 tablespoons dry cider or wine

5 tablespoons Japanese soy sauce

1 heaped tablespoon tomato purée

1 heaped teaspoon ground ginger

1 fat clove garlic, crushed

1 tablespoon light soft brown sugar

You will also need a
9 x 11 x 2 inches (23 x 28 x 5 cm) shallow roasting tin.

Pre-heat the oven to gas mark 6, 400°F (200°C).

These are a bit like spare ribs but without the bones - lovely and meaty and juicy. I like to serve them with brown rice.

First of all, make sure the strips of belly pork are absolutely dry by patting them with kitchen paper. Then rub each one all over with olive oil and season with freshly milled pepper (but no salt because of the sauce). Now pop them into the roasting tin, tucking the chopped onion in among them and sprinkling them with a few more drops of oil. Place the tin on the highest shelf in the oven and let them cook for 30 minutes. Meanwhile, make up the barbecue sauce simply by whisking all the sauce ingredients together until blended thoroughly.

When the pork has been cooking for 30 minutes, pour off any excess oil from the roasting tin, then pour the barbecue sauce over the pork and cook for a further 25 minutes, basting frequently.

Braised Pork with Prunes
Serves 4

1 lb 12 oz (800 g) belly pork, trimmed (trimmed weight 1 lb 8 oz/ 700 g), and cut into 1 inch (2.5 cm) pieces

4 oz (110 g) pitted Agen prunes, halved

1 tablespoon groundnut or other flavourless oil

6 juniper berries, crushed with the back of a spoon

½ teaspoon chopped fresh thyme

8 oz (225 g) onions, sliced

1 clove garlic, crushed

1 large Bramley cooking apple, peeled, cored and sliced

a little caster sugar

1 lb 8 oz (700 g) Desirée or King Edward potatoes, peeled and cut into ¾ inch (2 cm) slices

1 oz (25 g) butter

5 fl oz (150 ml) dry cider

salt and freshly milled black pepper

You will also need a large frying pan, a 7 x 12 x 2½ inch (18 x 30 x 6 cm), shallow, oval, ovenproof dish, and some foil.

Pre-heat the oven to gas mark 3, 325°F (170°C).

This is my version of a famous French classic with the addition of crisp potatoes on top, rather like a hotpot.

First of all, fry the pieces of pork in the oil in the frying pan so they brown nicely (you may need to do this in 2 batches), then arrange the pieces in the bottom of the ovenproof dish. Season with salt and freshly milled black pepper and sprinkle over the crushed juniper berries and chopped thyme. Now fry the onions and garlic a little bit (3-4 minutes) in the same pan, and scatter them round the pork with the pieces of prune tucked here and there.

Next, arrange the apple slices all over and give them a very slight dusting of caster sugar. Finally, arrange the potato slices on top, making them overlap one another. Season with some more pepper and salt, dot with a few flecks of butter and pour in the cider. Cover the dish with foil and bake for 1½ hours.

When the cooking time's up, remove the foil and cook for a further 50 minutes or so – or until the potatoes have turned a lovely golden brown.

Braised Meatballs in Goulash Sauce
Serves 4-6

1 lb 8 oz (700 g) minced pork

½ medium red pepper, deseeded and finely chopped

1 small onion, very finely chopped

1 fat clove garlic, crushed

2 tablespoons chopped fresh parsley

2 oz (50 g) white breadcrumbs

1 large egg, beaten

1 rounded tablespoon flour, seasoned with salt and freshly milled black pepper

2-3 tablespoons olive oil

salt and freshly milled black pepper

For the sauce

1 tablespoon olive oil

1 medium onion, chopped

½ medium red pepper, deseeded and finely chopped

1 clove garlic, crushed

1 rounded tablespoon hot Hungarian paprika, plus a little extra, to garnish

1 lb (450 g) ripe tomatoes, peeled and chopped, or 14 oz (400 g) tinned Italian chopped tomatoes

3½ fl oz (100 ml) crème fraîche

salt and freshly milled black pepper

You will also need a 6 pint (3.5 litre), lidded, flameproof casserole.

Pre-heat the oven to gas mark 1, 275°F (140°C).

This recipe never fails to please – minced pork together with pepper and onion is a wonderful combination of flavours. The meatballs are very light and the sauce rich and creamy. A classic Hungarian accompaniment would be buttered noodles tossed with poppy seeds – use 3 oz (75 g) tagliatelle per person, drained then tossed in ½ oz (10 g) butter and 1 teaspoon poppy seeds.

First, make the meatballs. Place the minced pork, chopped pepper, onion, garlic, parsley and breadcrumbs in a large bowl. Mix well, then add the egg and a good seasoning of salt and freshly milled black pepper. Now combine everything as thoroughly as possible, using either your hands or a large fork. Then take pieces of the mixture, about a tablespoon at a time, squeeze and roll each one into a small round – you should get 24 altogether – now coat each one lightly with seasoned flour (reserving any leftover flour for the sauce). Heat the 2 tablespoons of oil in the casserole and, when it's smoking hot, brown the meatballs a few at a time, transferring them to a plate as they are done, and adding a little more oil if you need it.

Next, make the sauce in the casserole. Heat the oil, add the onion and the red pepper together and cook over a medium heat for about 5 minutes, then add the garlic, cook for another minute, and stir in the paprika and any remaining bits of seasoned flour. Stir to soak up the juices, then add the tomatoes, season with salt and pepper, then bring it all up to simmering point, stirring all the time. Now add the meatballs to the sauce, bring back to simmering point, cover with a tight-fitting lid and transfer it to the middle shelf of the oven for 1½ hours. Just before serving, lightly stir in the crème fraîche to give a marbled effect. Spoon the meatballs on to freshly cooked noodles, or tagliatelle, and sprinkle a little extra paprika on as a garnish as they go to the table.

Spanish Pork with Potatoes and Olives
Serves 4-6

2 lb (900 g) shoulder of pork, trimmed and cut into bite-sized pieces

1 lb (450 g) salad or new potatoes, halved if large

1½ oz (40 g) black olives

1½ oz (40 g) green olives

1 lb (450 g) ripe, red tomatoes

2 tablespoons olive oil

2 medium onions, sliced into half-moon shapes

1 large red pepper, deseeded and sliced into 1¼ inch (3 cm) strips

2 cloves garlic, chopped

1 heaped teaspoon chopped fresh thyme, plus a few small sprigs

10 fl oz (275 ml) red wine

2 bay leaves

salt and freshly milled black pepper

You will also need a lidded, flameproof casserole with a capacity of 6 pints (3.5 litres).

Pre-heat the oven to gas mark 1, 275°F (140°C).

This is a more recent version of a recipe originally published in 1978 – the pork slowly braises in tomatoes and red wine, absorbing the flavour of the olives. Because I now cook potatoes in with it, all it needs is a green vegetable or a salad for a complete meal. I started off pitting the olives, but I now prefer them whole, as they look far nicer.

First, skin the tomatoes: pour boiling water over them and leave them for exactly 1 minute before draining and slipping off their skins (protecting your hands with a cloth, if necessary), then roughly chop them. Now heat 1 tablespoon of the oil in the casserole over a high heat, pat the cubes of pork with kitchen paper and brown them on all sides, about 6 pieces at a time, removing them to a plate as they're browned. Then, keeping the heat high, add the rest of the oil, then fry the onions and pepper to brown them a little at the edges – for about 6 minutes.

Now add the garlic, stir that around for about 1 minute, then return the browned meat to the casserole and add all the thyme, tomatoes, red wine, olives and bay leaves. Bring everything up to a gentle simmer, seasoning well, then put the lid on and transfer the casserole to the middle shelf of the oven for 1¼ hours. After that, add the potatoes, cover the pan again and cook for a further 45 minutes, or until the potatoes are tender.

Pork Chops Braised in Milk
Serves 4

4 large pork chops (at least
1 inch/2.5 cm thick)

4 tablespoons chopped
fresh parsley

2 tablespoons crushed
fresh rosemary, finely chopped

1 clove garlic, crushed

½ oz (10 g) butter

1 tablespoon groundnut or other
flavourless oil

1 medium onion, chopped small

2 stalks of celery, chopped small

8 oz (225 g) carrots, peeled and
chopped small

10 fl oz (275 ml) whole milk

salt and freshly milled
black pepper

You will also need a shallow,
flameproof casserole, with a
capacity of 6 pints (3.5 litres).

Pre-heat the oven to gas mark 4,
350°F, 180°C.

There has always been a connection between pigs and the dairy, as when cheese is made, the curds are separated from the whey and the whey is traditionally given to the pigs to flavour the meat. That's why I think this combination of pork and milk, invented in Italy, goes extremely well.

First of all, remove the skin from the chops, then cut a pocket in each one, slipping the knife in the fat side across towards the bone and making a slit about 2½ inches (6 cm) long. Then combine the chopped parsley and rosemary in a bowl and mix with the crushed garlic and some salt and freshly milled black pepper. Then push about 2 heaped teaspoonfuls of this herb mixture into each pocket. Now heat the butter and oil together in the casserole and fry the chops in 2 batches until lightly browned on both sides; remove the first batch to a plate before you fry the second.

Next, cook the prepared vegetables in the fat remaining in the casserole over a medium heat, stirring occasionally, for 5 minutes or until softened and golden, then return the chops, together with any juices, to the casserole. Pour in the milk, season, then bring the mixture up to simmering point and bake, uncovered, in the top part of the pre-heated oven for 1 hour-1 hour 15 minutes, or until the chops are cooked through and tender. The milk, by the way, is *supposed* to coagulate into a sauce.

Gammon
Bacon
Sausages

Pork Sausages in Red Wine
Serves 2-3

6 large, good-quality, pork
sausages (about 1 lb/450 g
in total)

10 fl oz (275 ml) red wine

1 dessertspoon olive oil

8 oz (225 g) streaky bacon
or pancetta, diced

1 large clove garlic

8 oz (225 g) shallots

1 dessertspoon juniper berries

1 teaspoon chopped fresh thyme

2 bay leaves

6 oz (175 g) medium, open-cap
mushrooms

1 heaped teaspoon plain flour

1 rounded teaspoon mustard
powder

1 oz (25 g) softened butter

1 rounded tablespoon good-quality
redcurrant jelly

salt and freshly milled
black pepper

You will also need a 4 pint
(2.25 litre), flameproof, lidded
casserole.

Bangers here are braised slowly with herbs, shallots, mushrooms and red wine. Then all you need is a dreamy pile of light, creamy mashed potato to go with them.

First, take the casserole and heat the oil in it. Then, with the heat at medium, brown the sausages evenly all over, taking care not to split the skins by turning them over too soon. Next, using a slotted spoon, transfer them to a plate while you brown the diced bacon, along with the garlic and shallots. Now crush the juniper berries very slightly without breaking them – just enough to release their flavour. Return the sausages to the casserole, pour in the wine and add the berries, then the thyme and bay leaves. Now season lightly, bring it all up to a gentle simmer, put a lid on the casserole, turn the heat as low as possible and let it all cook gently for 30 minutes.

After that, add the mushrooms, stirring them in well, then leave everything to cook gently for a further 20 minutes – this time without the lid so the liquid reduces slightly. To finish off, remove the sausages and vegetables to a warm serving dish, mix the flour and the mustard powder with the softened butter until you have a smooth paste and whisk this, a little at a time, into the casserole. Let everything bubble for a few more minutes, then take the casserole off the heat, return the sausages and vegetables to the casserole, whisk in the redcurrant jelly – and it's ready to serve.

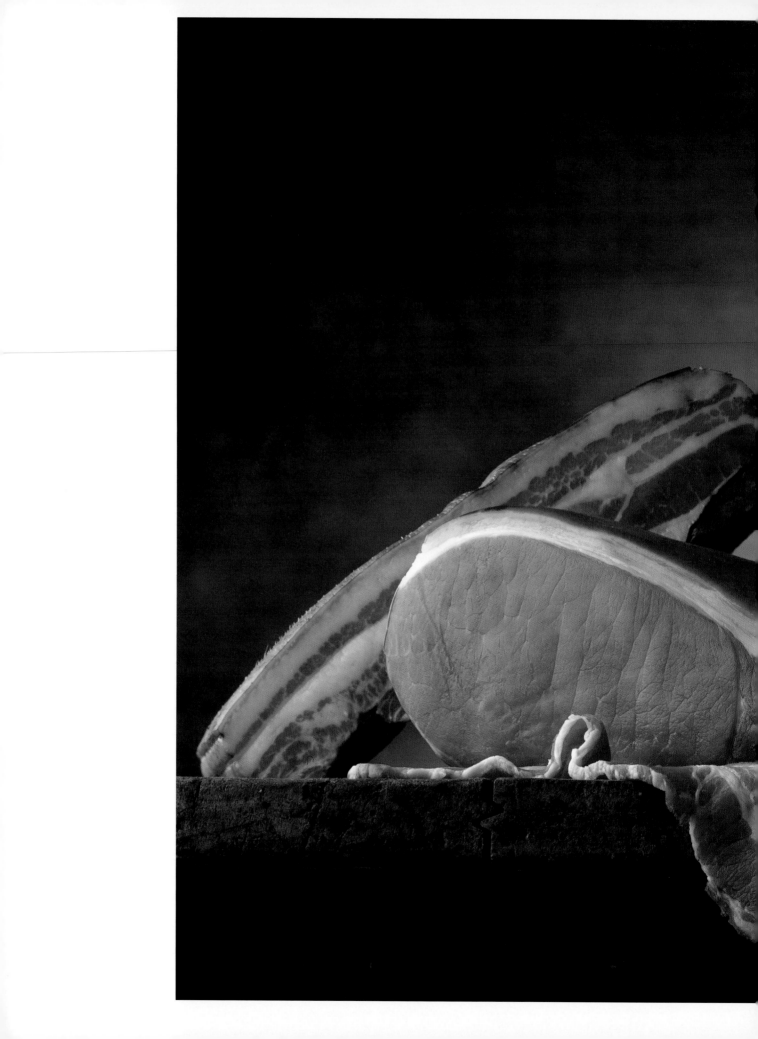

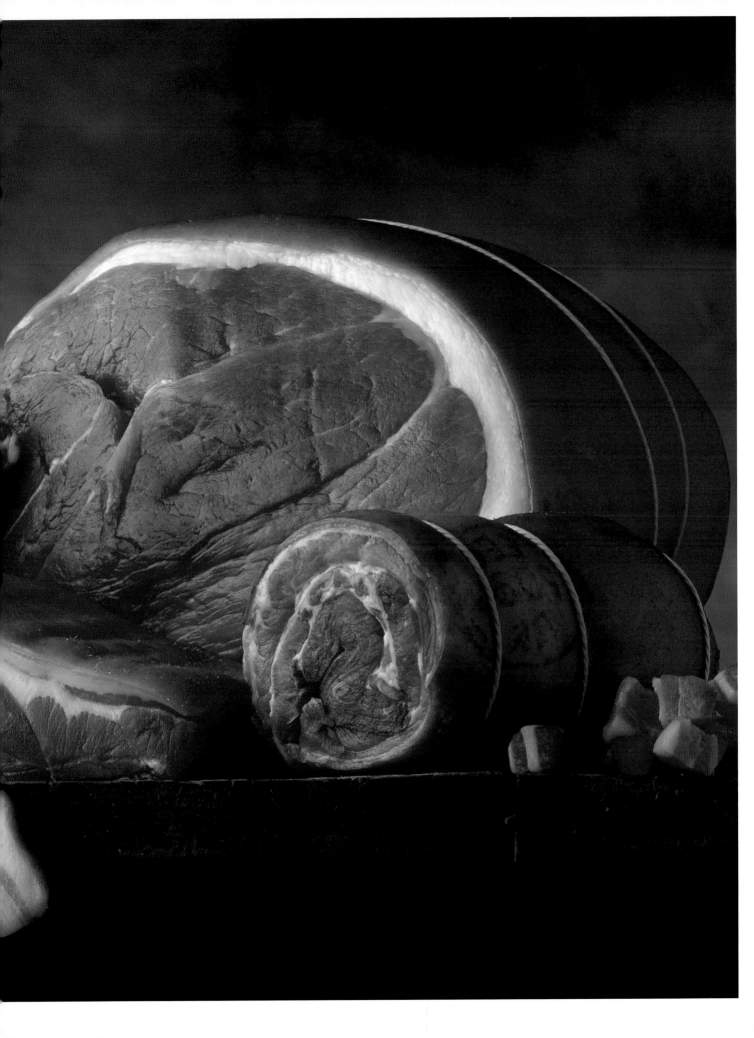

Boiled Bacon with Dumplings and Parsley Sauce
Serves 4

2 lb 8 oz (1.15 kg) boneless gammon joint or collar of bacon

2 bay leaves

a few parsley stalks

4 smallish onions, left whole

2 large carrots, scraped and cut in half

For the dumplings

4 oz (110 g) self-raising flour, plus a little extra for dusting

2 oz (50 g) shredded suet

2 tablespoons chopped fresh parsley

salt and freshly milled black pepper

For the parsley sauce

2 heaped tablespoons chopped fresh parsley

1 oz (25 g) butter

1 oz (25 g) plain flour

5 fl oz (150 ml) milk

10 fl oz (275 ml) stock (reserved from cooking the bacon)

1 teaspoon lemon juice

salt and freshly milled black pepper

You will also need a 6 pint (3.5 litre), flameproof, wide-bottomed, lidded casserole.

This is a really old English classic which is both filling and comforting on a cold day.

Begin by placing the gammon in the casserole with 3½ pints (2 litres) of water and add the bay leaves and parsley stalks. Then bring the water to the boil, put a lid on and simmer gently for 45 minutes. Next, add the peeled whole onions and halved carrots, replace the lid and continue simmering for a further 30 minutes.

Then, to make the dumplings, mix the flour, shredded suet and chopped parsley in a bowl, season with salt and black pepper, and add enough cold water (6-8 tablespoonfuls) to make a smooth, elastic dough. Transfer the dough to a lightly floured board and divide it into 12 small dumplings.

When the gammon's 30 minutes' cooking time is up, ladle out 10 fl oz (275 ml) of the stock into a measuring jug. Then, keeping the rest simmering, pop the dumplings in around the gammon – don't push them down, let them float – cover and cook for a further 25 minutes.

Meanwhile, make the parsley sauce. In a small saucepan, melt the butter and then, using a wooden spoon, stir in the flour till smooth, then add the milk, a little at a time, still stirring, followed by some of the reserved bacon stock, then switch to a balloon whisk and keep whisking after each addition. Now stir in the chopped parsley and lemon juice and season the sauce with salt and pepper and let it barely simmer for 5 minutes. Serve the gammon, cut in slices, with the onions, carrots and dumplings, and the sauce in a jug. Any leftover gammon is lovely cold.

Pork Sausages Braised in Cider with Apples and Juniper
Serves 3-4

6 large, good-quality pork
sausages (about 1 lb/450 g in total)

15 fl oz (425 ml) strong dry cider

1 tablespoon cider vinegar

1 Bramley cooking apple, cored
and sliced into rings (unpeeled)

1 Cox's apple, cored and sliced into
rings (unpeeled)

1 dessertspoon juniper berries,
crushed slightly, either in
a pestle and mortar or with the
back of a tablespoon

2 dessertspoons olive oil

8 oz (225 g) onions, sliced into
rings

1 large clove garlic, chopped

8 oz (225 g) lean smoked bacon,
roughly chopped

1 tablespoon plain flour

a few sprigs of fresh thyme

2 bay leaves

salt and freshly milled
black pepper

You will also need a large, heavy-
based frying pan, and a 4 pint
(2.25 litre), flameproof casserole,
with a tight-fitting lid.

Braised sausages seem to have turned up many times in my books over the years and, because I love them so much, here is yet another version – a lovely, comforting, warm, winter supper dish that needs copious amounts of fluffy mashed potato to spoon the sauce over. Crushing the juniper berries releases their lovely flavour.

Begin by taking the frying pan, place it on a medium heat and add 1 dessertspoon of the oil to it. As soon as it's hot, fry the sausages until they are nicely browned on all sides, then, using a draining spoon, transfer them to a plate. Now add the onions, garlic and bacon to the frying pan and cook these until they have also browned at the edges – about 10 minutes.

Meanwhile, place the casserole on to another heat source, again turned to medium, add the other dessertspoon of oil, then, when it's hot, add the apple rings and brown these on both sides, which will take 2-3 minutes. After that, add the sausages, followed by the bacon, onions and garlic, then sprinkle the flour in to soak up the juices, stirring it gently with a wooden spoon. Next, add the cider and cider vinegar, a little at a time, stirring after each addition. Then add the thyme, bay leaves and crushed juniper berries, season with salt and pepper, but not too much salt because of the bacon.

After that, put the lid on and simmer very gently on the lowest possible heat for 1 hour. Serve with mashed potato.

Gammon Steaks with White Wine and Gherkin Sauce
Serves 4

4 large gammon steaks
(7-8 oz/200-225 g each)

For the sauce

15 fl oz (425 ml) dry white wine

8 small gherkins, drained
and finely chopped

2 oz (50 g) butter

1 large onion, finely chopped

1 tablespoon plain flour

2 tablespoons chopped fresh
parsley

1 teaspoon lemon juice

salt and freshly milled
black pepper

This is best made with the small sharply flavoured gherkins, not the large fat dill cucumbers, and some sharp English mustard would go well with it.

First of all, pre-heat the grill to its highest setting and, while it's warming up, make the sauce. In a small saucepan melt the butter and soften the onion in it over a medium heat for 5 minutes, then stir in the flour and gradually add the wine, a little at a time, stirring after each addition until you have a smooth sauce. Turn the heat down to a low setting and let the sauce simmer for 10 minutes while you're cooking the gammon.

Remove the rind from the gammon steaks (the birds will love it chopped!), then snip the fat on the steaks with kitchen scissors at 1 inch (2.5 cm) intervals all round – this helps to keep it flat while it's cooking. Now, grill the gammon steaks for 2-3 minutes on each side, depending on the thickness of them.

Towards the end of the cooking time, stir the chopped gherkins, parsley and lemon juice into the sauce, then taste and season with pepper (but watch the salt because the gammon may be salty). Serve the gammon steaks with the sauce poured over.

Toad in the Hole with Roasted-onion Gravy
Serves 2-3

6 good-quality pork sausages
(about 1 lb/450 g in total)

1 tablespoon groundnut or other
flavourless oil, if needed

For the batter

3 oz (75 g) plain flour

1 large egg

3 fl oz (75 ml) semi-skimmed milk

salt and freshly milled
black pepper

For the onion gravy

8 oz (225 g) onion, sliced

2 teaspoons groundnut or other
flavourless oil

1 teaspoon caster sugar

1 dessertspoon Worcestershire
sauce

1 teaspoon mustard powder

15 fl oz (425 ml) vegetable stock

1 rounded dessertspoon plain flour

salt and freshly milled
black pepper

You will also need a solid-based,
flameproof roasting tin with a
base of 6 x 9 inches (15 x 23 cm),
2 inches (5 cm) deep, and a
baking tray, 10 x 14 inches
(25.5 x 35.5 cm).

Pre-heat the oven to gas mark 7,
425°F (220°C).

I can't give this high enough accolades – it's a simply wonderful creation from the humble origins of British cooking. If only you could order it in a restaurant, though. Can I persuade anyone? It is, after all, a sort of fusion food – a fusion of light, crispy, crunchy batter and plump, meaty pork sausages, all moistened with a generous amount of roasted-onion *jus*. Here's hoping!

Begin by making the batter, and to do this sift the flour into a large bowl, holding the sieve up high to give the flour a good airing. Now, with the back of a spoon, make a well in the centre, break the egg into it and add some salt and pepper. Now, measure the milk and 2 fl oz (55 ml) water in a measuring jug, then, using an electric hand whisk on a slow speed, begin to whisk the egg into the flour – as you whisk, the flour around the edges will slowly be incorporated. Then add the liquid gradually, stopping to scrape the flour into the mixture. Whisk until the batter is smooth. Now the batter is ready for use, and although it's been rumoured that batter left to stand is better, I have never found this, so just make it whenever it's convenient.

Now place the sliced onions for the gravy in a bowl, add 1 teaspoon of the oil and the sugar and toss the onions around to get the lightest coating, then spread them on the baking tray. Next, arrange the sausages in the roasting tin, then place the onions on a high shelf in the oven, with the sausages on a lower shelf, and set a timer for 10 minutes. When the timer goes off, remove the sausages from the oven but leave the onions in for a further 4-5 minutes – they need to be nicely blackened round the edges. When they are ready, remove them and leave to one side.

Now place the roasting tin containing the sausages over direct heat turned to medium and, if the sausages haven't released much fat, add the tablespoon of oil. When the tin is really hot and the oil is beginning to shimmer – it must be searing hot – quickly pour the batter in all around the sausages. Immediately return the roasting tin to the oven, this time on the highest shelf, and cook the whole thing for 30 minutes.

Now for the gravy. First, add the Worcestershire sauce and mustard powder to the stock, then add the onions from the baking tray to a medium pan. Now add the second teaspoon of oil, then, using a wooden spoon, stir in the plain flour. Stir all this together over a medium heat, then switch to a whisk and gradually add the stock to the pan, whisking all the time, until it's all in. Then bring it up to simmering point and gently simmer for 5 minutes. Taste to check the seasoning, then pour into a warmed serving jug. When the toad is ready, it should be puffed, brown and crisp, and the centre should look cooked and not too squidgy. Serve it immediately with the gravy, and it's absolutely wonderful with mashed potato.

The Delia Collection **Pork**

Frankfurters with Hot Potato Salad
Serves 4

8 large German frankfurters

1 lb 8 oz (700 g) Desirée or King Edward potatoes

6 tablespoons groundnut or other flavourless oil

1 medium onion, halved and thinly sliced

1 clove garlic, crushed

2 tablespoons cider vinegar

1 teaspoon English mustard

a few drops of Tabasco sauce

2 tablespoons chopped fresh parsley

salt and freshly milled black pepper

If you have a delicatessen in your area, try to get the really long frankfurters for this recipe, as they're generally much better than the supermarket variety.

Use a potato peeler to pare off the potato skins as thinly as possible, then cut the potatoes into even-sized chunks – not too small; if they are large, quarter them, and if they are small, halve them. Put the potato chunks in a steamer fitted over a large pan of boiling water, sprinkle a dessertspoon of salt all over them, put a lid on and steam the potatoes until they are absolutely tender – they should take 20-25 minutes. The way to tell whether they are ready is to pierce them with a skewer in the thickest part: they should not be hard in the centre. When the potatoes are cooked, remove them from the steamer, drain off the water, return them to the saucepan and cover with a clean tea cloth for about 4 minutes to absorb some of the steam.

While that's happening, heat 2 tablespoons of the oil in a frying pan and fry the onion and crushed garlic for 8-10 minutes or until softened. Next, add the remaining oil and the cider vinegar and stir in the mustard and Tabasco. Then season with salt and freshly milled black pepper, heat to simmering point and then turn the heat to low. At this stage, poach the frankfurters for 4-5 minutes (but check with the manufacturer's instructions for how long, because it does vary).

Next, put the potatoes into a warm serving bowl and pour over the oil and vinegar mixture. Now sprinkle with the parsley and, using a sharp knife, roughly chop the potatoes into smaller chunks. Then chop the hot cooked frankfurters into similar sized chunks and toss everything together. Have some extra mustard on the table.

Roast Collar of Bacon with Blackened Crackling with English Cumberland Sauce

Serves 6

5 lb (2.25 kg) smoked collar of bacon

1 tablespoon molasses or black treacle

sea salt

For the Cumberland sauce

1 medium lemon

1 medium orange

4 heaped tablespoons good-quality redcurrant jelly

4 tablespoons port

1 heaped teaspoon mustard powder

1 heaped teaspoon ground ginger

You will also need a solid, medium, shallow roasting tin.

Pre-heat the oven to gas mark 9, 475°F (240°C).

You could also use a prime gammon joint for this recipe. Scoring and painting the skin with molasses or black treacle turns it into superb crackling. Cumberland sauce is, for me, one of the great classic English sauces, provided it's made with a good-quality redcurrant jelly with a high fruit content. This is nice served with jacket potato wedges and braised red cabbage.

First of all, using a very sharp pointed knife, score the skin of the bacon in a criss-cross pattern, making little ½ inch (1 cm) diamonds (insert the tip of the knife only, hold the skin taut with one hand and drag the tip of the knife down in long movements).

To cook the bacon: warm the molasses or black treacle slightly (if it's very cold), then use a pastry brush to lightly coat all the little diamonds. Next, sprinkle the skin with salt crystals – pressing them well in – then place the joint in the roasting tin, skin side up (if it won't stand straight, use a couple of wodges of foil to prop it up).

Place the roasting tin in the oven and after 25 minutes turn the heat down to gas mark 4, 350°F (180°C) and continue to cook for a further 1¾-2 hours. It should feel tender all the way through when tested with a skewer.

To make the Cumberland sauce, first, thinly pare off the zest of both the lemon and the orange, using a potato peeler, then cut it into very small strips, ½ inch (1 cm) long and as thin as possible. Boil the strips in water in a small saucepan for 5 minutes to extract any bitterness, then drain well (throw away the water). Now place the redcurrant jelly in the saucepan with the port, and melt, whisking them together over a low heat for about 5 minutes. The redcurrant jelly won't melt completely, so it's best to sieve it afterwards to get rid of any obstinate little globules. In a bowl, mix the mustard and ginger with the juice of half the lemon until smooth, then add the juice of the orange, the port and redcurrant mixture and, finally, the strips of lemon and orange zest. Mix well and it's ready for use.

Leave the collar of bacon to rest for at least 30 minutes after coming out of the oven. Serve it with the English Cumberland Sauce.

Sausages with Puy Lentils
Serves 4

8 large, good-quality, herby, pork sausages (about 1 lb 5 oz/600 g in total)

6 oz (175 g) Puy lentils

1 large onion, chopped small

2 cloves garlic, crushed

1 oz (25 g) butter

2 tablespoons groundnut or other flavourless oil

14 oz (400 g) tinned chopped tomatoes

1 teaspoon granulated sugar

1 tablespoon chopped fresh thyme

1 bay leaf

salt and freshly milled black pepper

You will also need a 6 pint (3.5 litre), flameproof, lidded casserole.

Lentils have a great affinity with pork and sausages as they have the capacity to absorb the richness.

Begin by rinsing the lentils, then place them in a saucepan with $1\frac{3}{4}$ pints (1 litre) of water (don't add any salt), bring them to simmering point and cook gently for about 30 minutes, or until the lentils are tender but not disintegrating. Then drain them and keep the cooking liquid.

Meanwhile, fry the onion and garlic in the butter and 1 tablespoon of the oil in the casserole for 8-10 minutes to soften. Next, add the tinned tomatoes, sugar, thyme and bay leaf, and some salt and freshly milled black pepper, and let it all simmer gently (without a lid) until the liquid reduces and it becomes rather thick – you may need to stir it now and then and it will take about 5-7 minutes.

Now heat the remaining tablespoon of oil in a large frying pan and brown the sausages all over in it. Then, using a draining spoon, transfer them to the tomato mixture. Add the cooked lentils and 10 fl oz (275 ml) of the liquid they were cooked in. Stir well, then continue cooking over a very gentle heat for about 30 minutes – with a lid – and, if the mixture begins to look dry, add a little more liquid. Taste and add pepper and salt, if it needs it, before serving.

Boiled Smoked Bacon with Pease Pudding with Onion and Mustard Sauce
Serves 6

3 lb (1.35 kg) smoked collar of bacon, string removed

1 small onion, studded with a few whole cloves

2 bay leaves

1 small carrot, peeled

6 black peppercorns

For the pease pudding

6 oz (175 g) dried marrowfat peas (soaked overnight, then drained and the water discarded)

1 small onion, quartered

1 bay leaf

1 sprig of fresh thyme

1 oz (25 g) butter

1 large egg, beaten

freshly grated nutmeg

salt and freshly milled black pepper

For the onion and mustard sauce

1 large onion, chopped small

1 rounded teaspoon mustard powder

1 rounded teaspoon wholegrain mustard

1½ oz (40 g) butter

1 oz (25 g) plain flour

6 fl oz (175 ml) milk

6 fl oz (175 ml) stock (reserved from cooking the bacon)

salt and freshly milled black pepper

Let me explain the appeal of this delightfully unfashionable, totally forgotten delicacy. First, collar of bacon has more flavour than the leaner, middle-cut gammon. Secondly, I'm sure many people have forgotten – or never actually tasted – dried marrowfat peas with their mealy texture and concentrated flavour of peas. Then, when we add an onion and mustard sauce, the combination of the whole is utterly sublime.

Start off by cooking the pease pudding. To do this, place the soaked and drained peas in a pan, pour in just enough water to cover, then add the onion, bay leaf and thyme (but no salt). Bring it up to a gentle simmer, put the lid on and cook for about 1 hour, or until the skins split and the peas are tender – they will be having some more cooking so they don't need to be absolutely smashed.

Now drain off the cooking water, discarding the thyme and bay leaf, then put the peas and the onion into a bowl and mash them with a large fork, along with the butter, beaten egg and a seasoning of salt and pepper, plus a few good gratings of nutmeg. Now transfer the mashed pea mixture to sit in the centre of the square of muslin, gather the edges into the centre then, leaving a bit of room for it to expand, tie it securely with string, leaving enough spare to tie it to the handle of the pan.

What you need to do now is place the bacon in the casserole, along with the small onion studded with cloves, the bay leaves, carrot and peppercorns, then tie the pudding to the handle of the pan so that it sits alongside the bacon in the casserole. Cover with cold water and bring the whole lot up to a gentle simmer. Put a lid on and let it cook very gently for 1¼ hours.

When the bacon is cooked, transfer it to a dish, cover with foil and let it rest. Leave the pudding in the casserole but ladle out 6 fl oz (175 ml) of the cooking liquid into a measuring jug. You can freeze the rest to use as stock in soups.

Next, make up the sauce: in a smallish saucepan, melt 1 oz (25 g) of the butter and add the onion and, when you've stirred it so it's nice and buttery, let it cook on the lowest possible heat for about 20 minutes. It's important not to let it colour, so

You will also need a 6 pint (3.5 litre), lidded, flameproof casserole, a 12 inch (30 cm) square piece of muslin and some string.

give it a few stirs from time to time. Now, using a wooden spoon, stir in the flour and the powdered mustard till smooth, then add the milk, a little at a time, still stirring, followed by some of the bacon stock, then switch to a balloon whisk and keep whisking after each addition. Now taste and season the sauce with salt and pepper and let it barely simmer for 5 minutes. After that, stir in the wholegrain mustard and the rest of the butter, then pour into a warmed serving jug.

Carve the bacon joint into slices and cut slices of the pease pudding (rather as you would do with a cake) and have some extra mustard on the table. I serve this with mashed potato and boiled buttered Savoy cabbage, but smaller steamed potatoes, such as Anya or Charlotte, would be good.

Braised Sausages with Borlotti Beans, Rosemary and Sage
Serves 2-3

6 large, good-quality, meaty pork sausages (1 lb/450 g in total)

8 oz (225 g) dried borlotti beans

1 heaped teaspoon chopped fresh rosemary, plus 2-3 sprigs to garnish

1 heaped teaspoon chopped fresh sage, plus 2-3 leaves to garnish

1 tablespoon olive oil

4 oz (110 g) sliced smoked pancetta or smoked bacon, chopped

1 large red onion, chopped

2 cloves garlic, crushed

10 fl oz (275 ml) dry white wine

salt and freshly milled black pepper

You will also need a lidded, flameproof casserole with a capacity of 4 pints (2.25 litres).

Pre-heat the oven to gas mark 1, 275°F (140°C).

You can use cannellini beans in this recipe, but borlotti are the best of all. The smokiness of the pancetta is also important, but if you can't get it, use smoked bacon.

First of all, soak the borlotti beans. Wash them under cold, running water and discard any broken ones or alien bits. Then, if it is convenient, soak them overnight in 4 pints (2.25 litres) cold water. If you haven't the time for this, simply bring them up to the boil (using the same quantity of water), boil for 10 minutes and leave them to soak for 2 hours. Either way, drain the beans, reserving the soaking liquid.

Heat the oil in the casserole over a medium heat and carefully brown the sausages, turning them occasionally so they are a nice golden brown colour on all sides – this will take 8-10 minutes.

After that, remove them to a plate, then add the pancetta to the frying pan, turn up the heat and toss it around for about 5 minutes, or until it's golden brown at the edges. Now, using a draining spoon, transfer it to join the sausages, then turn the heat down again to medium and soften the onion for 10 minutes in the juices left in the pan, stirring it around from time to time. Then add the garlic and cook for another minute. Next, add the drained beans to the casserole, along with the herbs, then the sausages and pancetta, tucking them in among the beans, and finally, add the wine and 10 fl oz (275 ml) of the reserved water. Season with salt and freshly milled black pepper and bring everything up to simmering point on the hob. Now put a lid on the casserole and transfer it to the centre shelf of the oven to cook slowly for 3 hours. Serve, garnished with the sprigs of rosemary and sage leaves.

I don't think this needs any other vegetable but a green salad, and some Italian cheese would be nice to follow.

Bacon and Egg Pies
Makes 12

4 rashers back bacon, derinded

3 large eggs

about 4 fl oz (120 ml) milk, plus
a little extra for brushing
the top of the pies

salt and freshly milled
black pepper

For the shortcrust pastry

6 oz (175 g) plain flour, plus a little
extra for dusting

a pinch of salt

1½ oz (40 g) softened lard

1½ oz (40 g) softened butter

You will also need a 12 hole patty
tin, each hole 1¾ inches (4.5 cm) at
the base, 2½ inches (6 cm) at the
top, and ¾ inch (2 cm) deep, well
greased, plus a 3½ inch (9 cm)
and a 3 inch (7.5 cm) pastry cutter.

Home-made individual bacon and egg pies, baked in patty tins or as a whole pie, make a very good and easily transportable picnic dish. Alternatively, they are nice served warm after the picnic if the weather wasn't up to scratch. For a whole pie, use an 8 inch (20 cm) tin, 4 eggs, 6 rashers of back bacon and 5 fl oz (150 ml) of milk.

Begin by making the pastry by sifting the flour and pinch of salt into a large bowl, holding the sieve as high as possible. Now add the lard and butter, cut into smallish lumps, then take a knife and begin to cut the fat into the flour. Go on doing this until it looks fairly evenly blended, then begin to rub the fat into the flour, using your fingertips only, and being as light as possible. As you do this, lift it up high and let it fall back into the bowl, just long enough to make the mixture crumbly with a few odd lumps here and there. Now sprinkle 1 tablespoon of water in, then, with a knife, start bringing the dough together. Then discard the knife and, finally, bring it together with your fingertips. When enough liquid is added, the pastry should leave the bowl fairly clean. If this hasn't happened, then add a spot more water. Now place the pastry in a polythene bag and leave it in the fridge for 30 minutes to rest.

Next, hardboil 2 of the eggs by placing them in a small saucepan and adding enough water to cover them by about ½ inch (1 cm). Bring the water up to simmering point and put a timer on for 7 minutes. Then, when the time is up, cool the eggs rapidly under cold, running water for about a minute, and leave them in cold water till they're cool. Meanwhile, grill (or fry) the bacon gently until the fat begins to run and pre-heat the oven to gas mark 6, 400°F (200°C). Roll out half of the pastry, on a lightly floured surface, cut out 12 rounds using the 3½ inch (9 cm) cutter and line the patty tin. Now peel and chop the eggs quite small and chop the bacon fairly small, too, Then divide the egg and bacon among the pies and season with freshly milled pepper and a very little salt. Beat the remaining egg together with the milk and carefully pour the mixture into the pies, allowing it to settle as you go. Dampen the edges and roll out the rest of the pastry to cut out the smaller rounds for the lids. Make a small hole in the centre of each pie, brush the tops with milk, then bake for 10 minutes. After that, reduce the heat to gas mark 5, 375°F (190°C) and cook for a further 25 minutes.

Baked Sugar-glazed Whole Gammon
Serves 20-25

2 heaped tablespoons demerara
sugar

1 whole gammon
(12-14 lb/5.4-6.3 kg)

about 24 whole cloves

2 tablespoons English mustard

You will also need a large
roasting tin, 11 x 16 x 2 inches
(28 x 40 x 5 cm), and some extra
wide kitchen foil.

Pre-heat the oven to gas mark 3,
325°F (170°C).

This is an alternative way of serving gammon and I like it served with English Cumberland Sauce (see page 88).

Soak the gammon according to the supplier's instructions. Then tear off 2 very large pieces of foil and arrange one lengthways and the other widthways over the roasting tin. Place the gammon in the centre and bring the widthways piece of foil up first and seal the two ends together by folding over to form a kind of pleat. This should be done loosely so there is room for air to circulate around the gammon. Now bring the lengthways pieces up at each end and carefully fold these to seal what is now a tent of foil.

Place the gammon in the oven and let it bake for 20 minutes per pound (450 g) – that is 4 hours for a 12 lb (5.4 kg) piece or 4 hours 40 minutes for a 14 lb (6.3 kg) piece. About 30 minutes before the end of the cooking time, remove the gammon and increase the heat to gas mark 7, 425°F (220°C). Open up the foil and transfer the gammon to a work surface (with help!). Now drain off all the juices (and reserve these in a bowl: the bacon fat will solidify and can be used for frying and the jelly for enriching lentil or pea soups).

Next, peel off all the skin – make a couple of horizontal incisions and you should be able to peel it off in strips, using a cloth to protect your hands from the heat. Now score the fat with criss-cross cuts, making a diamond pattern. Stud a clove into the centre of each diamond shape, then smother the mustard all over, using a palette knife to spread it evenly. Finally, sprinkle the sugar all over and press it in with your hands. Return the gammon to the tin and bake for a further 30 minutes or until it is a glazed, golden mahogany colour (cover the gammon loosely with foil towards the end of the cooking time if it is starting to brown too much).

If the gammon is to be served hot, leave it to rest for about 45 minutes before carving. If cold, leave it to cool slowly overnight in a cool place, then refrigerate.

Other Pork Dishes

Picnic Pork Pie
Serves 4-6

8 oz (225 g) chump end of pork, trimmed and chopped into ½ inch (1 cm) cubes

8 oz (225 g) best end of veal, trimmed and chopped into ½ inch (1 cm) cubes (if you can't get veal, use all pork)

4 slices smoked streaky bacon, derinded and diced

1 medium potato (7 oz/200 g), peeled and chopped into ¾ inch (2 cm) cubes

1 small clove garlic, crushed

¼ teaspoon dried thyme

¼ teaspoon ground allspice

1 tablespoon vegetable stock (or water)

1 dessertspoon chopped fresh parsley

1 small egg, lightly beaten, to glaze

salt and freshly milled black pepper

For the shortcrust pastry

6 oz (175 g) plain flour, plus a little extra for dusting

a pinch of salt

1½ oz (40 g) softened lard

1½ oz (40 g) softened butter

You will also need a tin that has a rim and sloping sides, 1½ inches (4 cm) deep, with a 7 inch (18 cm) base and a ½ inch (1 cm rim), lightly greased, and a medium, solid baking sheet.

The reason this pie is great for a picnic is that it stays beautifully moist and is so easy to slice and serve.

Begin by making the pastry by sifting the flour and pinch of salt into a large bowl, holding the sieve as high as possible. Now add the lard and butter, cut into smallish lumps, then take a knife and begin to cut the fat into the flour. Go on doing this until it looks fairly evenly blended, then begin to rub the fat into the flour using your fingertips only and being as light as possible. As you do this, lift it up high and let it fall back into the bowl, just long enough to make the mixture crumbly with a few odd lumps here and there. Now sprinkle 1 tablespoon of water in, then, with a knife, start bringing the dough together. Then discard the knife and, finally, bring the dough together with your fingertips. When enough liquid is added, the pastry should leave the bowl fairly clean. If this hasn't happened, then add a spot more water. Now place the pastry in a polythene bag and leave it in the fridge for 30 minutes to rest. Pre-heat the oven to gas mark 6, 400°F (200°C) and pop the baking sheet in to pre-heat at the same time.

Next, place the chopped meats and bacon in a mixing bowl and add all the other ingredients (except the beaten egg). Now, mix them all thoroughly together, with a good seasoning of salt and pepper. Then divide the pastry in half, and roll out one half, on a lightly floured surface, to line the tin. Pile the meat mixture evenly on the pastry, dampen the edges, then roll out the rest of the pastry to form a lid and fit it over the filling, sealing well all round, trimming and pinching (or fluting) the edges. Make a small hole in the centre of the lid and, if you have time, you can use the trimmings to make a few leaves for decoration. Now brush the pie with the beaten egg, place it on the baking sheet in the oven, then after 10 minutes reduce the heat to gas mark 4, 350°F (180°C) and bake for a further 45 minutes. If the pastry gets a bit too brown during cooking, cover it with foil. Allow the pie to cool, then wrap it (plate as well) in a double thickness of foil ready to take on the picnic.

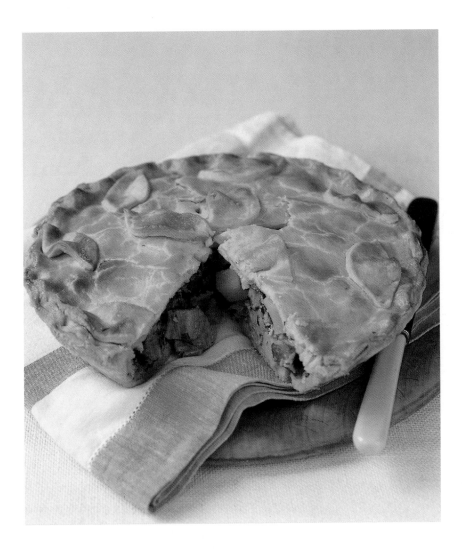

Chorizo Hash with Red Pepper and Paprika
Serves 2

5 oz (150 g) chorizo sausage

1 small red pepper

1 rounded teaspoon hot paprika

1 medium onion

10 oz (275 g) Desirée or King Edward potatoes

4 tablespoons olive oil

1 fat clove garlic, crushed

2 large, very fresh eggs

salt and freshly milled black pepper

You will also need a heavy-based frying pan, about 8 inches (20 cm) in diameter, a slightly smaller frying pan for the eggs, and 2 plates placed in a warming oven.

This, if you like, is a more sophisticated version of corned-beef hash with fried eggs, using red peppers as well as onion and potato. It's brilliant, but only worth making if you get genuine Spanish chorizo made in Spain, available at deli counters and specialist food shops – the English 'made in Surbiton'-type clones are not at all what they should be.

First, the onion needs to be peeled, sliced in half and then each half sliced as thinly as possible, so you end up with little half-moon shapes. Next, halve and deseed the red pepper, slice it, then chop it into $\frac{1}{2}$ inch (1 cm) pieces. After that, peel the skin off the chorizo sausage and cut it into pieces roughly the same size as the pepper.

The potatoes need to be washed and cut into $\frac{1}{2}$ inch (1 cm) cubes, leaving the skin on. Then place them in a saucepan and pour enough boiling water from the kettle to almost cover them, then add salt and a lid and simmer for just 5 minutes before draining them in a colander and covering with a clean tea cloth to absorb the steam.

Next, heat 2 tablespoons of the oil in the larger frying pan and, when it's fairly hot, add the onion, pepper and garlic and cook for about 6 minutes, until softened and tinged brown at the edges. Then push these to the side of the pan, add the chorizo and, keeping the heat fairly high, cook for about 2 minutes, again, till nicely browned at the edges. Next, add the paprika and stir everything together, then remove the whole lot to a plate. Now add another tablespoon of oil to the pan and, still keeping the heat high, add the potatoes and seasoning. Toss them around in the hot pan for about 3 minutes, keeping them moving, until they begin to crisp and brown at the edges, then return the chorizo, onion and pepper to the pan and, using a pan slice, keep turning the mixture over. Carry on cooking the whole thing for 5-6 minutes, until it's all really brown and crispy. Then turn the heat down to its lowest setting and, in the other pan, fry the eggs in the remaining oil. Serve the hash divided between the two warmed plates with an egg on top of each and have plenty of tomato ketchup on the table.

American Meatloaf with Red Onion, Tomato and Chilli Relish
Serves 8

1 lb (450 g) minced pork (not too lean)

1 lb (450 g) minced beef

2 medium onions

2 cloves garlic, peeled

3 heaped tablespoons chopped fresh parsley

1 dessertspoon chopped fresh thyme

1 large egg

3 oz (75 g) white bread, sliced and crusts removed, cut into 1 inch (2.5 cm) cubes

3 tablespoons milk

1½ rounded teaspoons English mustard powder

2 tablespoons Worcestershire sauce

4 fl oz (120 ml) dry white wine

about 8 slices (6 oz/175 g) smoked streaky bacon

salt and freshly milled black pepper

For the red onion, tomato and chilli relish

1 medium red onion, peeled and finely chopped

1 lb (450 g) ripe red tomatoes

1 small red chilli, deseeded and finely chopped

1 large clove garlic, peeled and crushed

2 tablespoons dark brown soft sugar

Serve this hot on a cold winter's day with some buttery jacket potatoes or, if the weather is warm, it's lovely served cold with salads and chutney or pickles. You can take thick chunks to serve with crusty bread on a picnic, and any leftover meatloaf is wonderful in sandwiches for a lunch box.

The best way to make this meatloaf is in a large food processor, if you've got one. In which case you can begin by chopping the onions, garlic, parsley and thyme all together until the onion is very finely chopped, then add the meats and break in the egg. Place the bread in a little bowl, spoon the milk over, then mix it with your hands or a fork until the bread has broken down to fine crumbs. Add these to the processor, along with the mustard powder, Worcestershire sauce, wine and a really good seasoning of salt and pepper. Now, switching on and off, or using the pulse button, mix the whole lot together until thoroughly blended. If you don't have a food processor, grate or mince the onion, chop the garlic finely, then mix everything thoroughly in a large bowl.

When the mixture is ready, pack it into the loaf tin and smooth the top with the back of a spoon, then snip the rind off the bacon and lay the slices all along the top of the meat, slightly overlapping, and press them down firmly. Now place a piece of foil over the top and twist or pleat the corners. Stand the tin in the roasting tin, pour about 1½ inches (4 cm) boiling water into the roasting tin straight from the kettle and place the whole thing on the middle shelf of the oven. Let it cook slowly for 2 hours; you may need to top up the water halfway through cooking.

To make the relish, first you need to skin the tomatoes, so pour boiling water over them and leave for exactly 1 minute before draining them and slipping off the skins (protect your hands with a cloth if they are too hot). Put the onion, chilli, garlic and tomatoes in a food processor and blend until finely chopped, then place the mixture in a small saucepan and add the sugar and vinegar. Place the pan over a gentle heat and simmer very gently, without a lid, for 2 hours, by which time the mixture will have reduced to a thick sauce. Towards the end of the cooking time, stir frequently so the sauce doesn't stick to the bottom of the pan. Then taste to check the seasoning. When

8 fl oz (225 ml) balsamic
vinegar

salt and freshly milled
black pepper

You will also need a 2 lb (900 g)
loaf tin, 4¾ x 7½ x 3½ inches
(12 x 19 x 9 cm) deep, preferably
non-stick, a small, shallow roasting
tin, and some kitchen foil.

Pre-heat the oven to gas mark 2,
300°F (150°C).

the meatloaf has had its 2 hours' cooking, remove the foil and insert a skewer into the meat loaf; press the skewer down to make sure that the juices are running clear.

Now, if the meatloaf is cooked, remove it from the oven then let it cool for about 30 minutes and after that, if you're serving it cold, replace the foil and place something heavy on top to weigh it down. Leave it weighted like this until it's completely cold. This makes the meatloaf easier to slice. If you're serving the meatloaf hot, just allow it to rest for 30 minutes in the tin, covered with foil, then turn it out on to a board and serve, cut in slices. The relish can be served hot or cold.

Sausage Rolls with Sage and Onion
Makes 24

14 oz (400 g) good-quality pork sausagemeat or sausages

1 tablespoon chopped fresh sage

1 small onion, very finely chopped

plain flour for dusting

½ x 375 g pack fresh ready-rolled puff pastry, or same quantity ready-made puff pastry in a block

1 large egg, beaten

salt and freshly milled black pepper

You will also need a large baking sheet, lightly greased.

Pre-heat the oven to gas mark 6, 400°F (200°C).

These are our once-a-year treat at home at Christmas, which for me is a time to forget all about fiddly canapés. My resounding answer as to what to serve with Christmas drinks or offer to unexpected callers is to do what my mother and grandmother did, and that is to hand round a plate of warm, bite-sized sausage rolls with some crunchy pickled onions and celery.

On a well-floured surface, using a well-floured rolling pin, roll the pastry out to an oblong measuring 10 x 12 inches (25.5 x 30 cm), then cut the pastry lengthways into 2 oblongs, 5 x 12 inches (13 x 30 cm). You need to do this even if you are using ready-rolled puff pastry as it won't be rolled thinly enough for this recipe.

Now combine the sausagemeat, sage and onion with a really good seasoning of salt and pepper (if you're using sausages, just slit the skins lengthways and peel them off). Now place the sausagemeat mixture on a separate surface or board, divide it into 2, then, using your hands, simply roll out each half into a long sausage shape the same length as the pastry strips (just keep going, it will eventually roll out).

Now place the sausagemeat rolls on to the pastry strips, dampen one long edge of each strip with some of the beaten egg (using a pastry brush), then roll them up. Seal the edges well and turn the rolls over so the sealed seam is underneath. Next, use a very sharp knife to cut the sausage rolls into 1 inch (2.5 cm) lengths, and then a pair of scissors to make 2 snips in the top of each little roll (to allow the steam to escape). Now brush each one with beaten egg, then line them up on the baking sheet and bake in the centre of the oven for 20-25 minutes. Cool on a wire rack and, when cold, store them between layers of baking parchment in airtight containers.

Devilled Spare Ribs
Serves 4

3 lb (1.35 kg) meaty spare ribs

2 tablespoons groundnut or other flavourless oil

freshly milled black pepper

For the sauce

2 fat cloves garlic

2 teaspoons salt

10 fl oz (275 ml) red wine

2 tablespoons Worcestershire sauce

2 tablespoons red wine vinegar

2 rounded tablespoons tomato purée

2 rounded teaspoons English mustard powder

2 teaspoons runny honey

2 teaspoons freshly grated ginger

1 teaspoon ground ginger

You will also need a shallow roasting tin, about 10 x 14 inches (25.5 x 35.5 cm), in which the ribs will fit comfortably in a single layer.

Pre-heat the oven to gas mark 4, 350°F (180°C).

Now it's so easy to buy thick, meaty spare ribs, you can make this doddle of a recipe in no time at all. The sauce takes about 5 minutes and the rest all happens in the oven.

First of all, lay the ribs in the base of the tin, brushing them with oil and seasoning with black pepper. Then make the sauce by simply crushing the garlic with the salt to a paste, using a pestle and mortar, then whisking it together with all the other ingredients – use a balloon whisk and it will all be amalgamated in moments.

Pour the sauce all over the ribs, making sure each one gets a good coating. Then pop them on to the highest shelf of the oven, bake them for 45 minutes, then give them all a basting and cook for a further 25 minutes.

Serve the ribs with the lovely thick reduced sauce spooned over, and I think they are very good served with some rice and a salad.

Faggots and Mushy Peas
Serves 4

4 oz (110 g) unsmoked bacon, bought in one piece, then cut into 1 inch (2.5 cm) cubes

6 oz (175 g) pigs' liver, cut into 1 inch (2.5 cm) cubes

1 lb (450 g) trimmed fat belly pork, cut into 1 inch (2.5 cm) cubes

2 medium onions, quartered

15 fl oz (425 ml) vegetable stock

2 oz (50 g) fresh white breadcrumbs

1 teaspoon chopped fresh thyme

1 teaspoon chopped fresh sage

¼ teaspoon ground mace

salt and freshly milled black pepper

For the mushy peas

12 oz (350 g) green split peas

1 teaspoon tomato purée

1 teaspoon Worcestershire sauce

1 dessertspoon mushroom ketchup, if available

1 medium onion, quartered

2 oz (50 g) butter

salt and freshly milled black pepper

You will also need a small (4 pint/2.25 litre), lidded casserole, and an 8 x 12 x 2 inch (20 x 30 x 5 cm), shallow baking dish, lightly greased.

Pre-heat the oven to gas mark 5, 375°F (190°C).

A real old-fashioned treat – traditionally served with 'mushy' peas. You can, if you prefer, increase the liver and reduce the pork and bacon.

First of all, place the cubes of bacon, liver and pork in the casserole, along with the quartered onions, then pour in the stock. Cover the casserole and cook in the centre of the oven for 45 minutes, then drain the meat and onions in a sieve (reserving the liquid) and leave until cold. Next, place the meat and onions in a food processor and process until finely chopped, then add the breadcrumbs, herbs and mace. Season with salt and pepper, and whiz again to combine everything thoroughly. Next, use your hands to shape the mixture into 8 good-sized balls.

Now arrange the faggots in a single layer in the baking dish. Pour over 10 fl oz (275 ml) of the reserved liquid and bake (uncovered) on a high shelf of the oven for 45 minutes.

To cook the peas, mix the tomato purée, Worcestershire sauce and mushroom ketchup (if using) with 1¼ pints (725 ml) water, and pour this into a pan, adding the onion quarters. Bring to the boil, then add the split peas and bring back to the boil. Now turn the heat down, cover the pan and simmer gently for 45-60 minutes, or until the peas are absolutely tender; you may need to add a little more hot water towards the end of the cooking time. After that, mash the butter into the split peas, along with a seasoning of salt and pepper. Serve the faggots with the mushy peas, and the juices poured over.

Pork Kebabs with Honey and Ginger
Serves 4

1 lb 8 oz (700 g) pork fillet

2 medium onions, peeled

5 pieces of preserved stem ginger in syrup, drained (reserve 2 tablespoons of the syrup for the marinade)

4 fl oz (120 ml) dry white wine

For the marinade

1 tablespoon runny honey

6 fl oz (175 ml) groundnut or other flavourless oil

4 tablespoons dry white wine

1 dessertspoon cider vinegar,

1 dessertspoon ground ginger

2 cloves garlic, crushed

2 tablespoons stem ginger syrup (reserved from the preserved stem ginger)

salt and freshly milled black pepper

You will also need 4 wooden bamboo skewers, 12 inches (30 cm) long. Alternatively, use metal skewers.

If you have to work and cook, you can leave this little lot to marinade in the morning and just pop them under the grill when you get home. These are also nice served with a sharp spiced apple sauce (see page 128).

First, cut the meat into roughly 1 inch (2.5 cm) cubes, leaving any fat on. Then combine all the ingredients for the marinade together in a large bowl and whisk to blend them thoroughly. Season well with salt and freshly milled black pepper, then add the cubes of meat and stir well to coat in the marinade. Cover and leave in a cool place to marinate for about 6 to 8 hours.

If you have wooden skewers, you need to soak them for 30 minutes in hot water before cooking (to prevent them burning). When you are ready to cook the kebabs, pre-heat the grill to its highest setting. Then, to assemble them, cut each of the onion into sixths through the root. Then thinly slice the stem ginger pieces and thread alternate pieces of meat, onion and preserved ginger on to the skewers. Grill them for 15-20 minutes and don't worry if they look a bit black – they taste fine. Brush occasionally with the marinade and turn the kebabs 2 or 3 times while they are cooking. When they are cooked, remove the kebabs to a plate and cover to keep warm. Then, make a sauce by adding the 4 fl oz (120 ml) of dry white wine to the grill pan juices, along with any remaining marinade, and boiling over direct heat till syrupy.

Coarse Country Pâté
Serves 10-12

1 lb (450 g) pork streaky rashers, with as much fat as possible

10 oz (275 g) dry-cured, smoked streaky bacon

12 oz (350 g) shoulder of veal

8 oz (225 g) pigs' liver

20 juniper berries

20 whole black peppercorns

1 heaped teaspoon salt

¼ rounded teaspoon ground mace

2 large cloves garlic, crushed

1 heaped teaspoon chopped fresh thyme

4 fl oz (120 ml) dry white wine

1 fl oz (25 ml) brandy

To decorate

fresh bay leaves

a few extra juniper berries

You will also need a terrine with a 3 pint (1.75 litre) capacity, or a 2 lb (900 g) loaf tin, a roasting tin and some foil.

If you long to eat some of the rough country pâté available all over France, but in short supply here, why not make some? You won't believe how blissfully easy it is, and using a processor instead of buying the meat ready-minced, makes it coarser and chunkier. Serve it for lunch with a side salad or watercress, some crisp cornichons and chargrilled or toasted country bread and, if you close your eyes, you're in France! Warning! Don't be tempted to buy lean meat – the presence of fat is essential. What happens is that as it cooks it will dissolve and surround the pâté, and although you won't be eating it, it is essential for keeping the pâté moist.

You'll find it's best to process the different meats one at a time (finishing with the pigs' liver, as this is the messiest). Begin by cutting the meats into rough pieces, then place them in the food processor bowl and process until quite finely chopped. Next, tip each meat in turn into a large mixing bowl and mix them together very thoroughly. Now coarsely crush first the juniper berries and then the black peppercorns in a pestle and mortar and add these to the meat, along with the heaped teaspoon of salt, the mace, garlic and thyme. Now you need to mix again even more thoroughly to distribute all the flavours evenly. After this, add the wine and brandy and give it a final mix, then cover the bowl with a cloth and leave it in a cool place for a couple of hours to allow the flavours to be absorbed.

Before cooking the pâté, pre-heat the oven to gas mark 2, 300°F (150°C). Then pack the mixture into the terrine or loaf tin and decorate the top with the bay leaves and the extra juniper berries. Place the terrine or tin in a roasting tin half-filled with hot water on the centre shelf of the oven and leave it there for about 1¾ hours. By the time it has cooked, the pâté will have shrunk quite a bit. Remove it from the oven and allow it to cool without draining off any of the surrounding juices; once the pâté has cooled, the surrounding fat and jelly will keep it beautifully moist.

When the pâté is cold, place a double strip of foil across the top and put a few weights on to press it down for at least a few hours – this pressing isn't essential but it helps to make the pâté less crumbly if you want to serve it in slices. If you don't have any scale weights, use any heavy object: bricks, tins of food or any innovation you can think of instead. (If you don't weight it, you can serve it in chunks rather than slices.) Then, place the pâté, weights and all, into the fridge overnight.

To serve the pâté you need to take it out of the fridge at least 30 minutes ahead, to return it to room temperature, then turn it out of the terrine or loaf tin and remove the surrounding jelly and any fat. Slice and serve with cornichons, watercress and hot toasted or chargrilled bread, or some very crusty, fresh bread.

For chargrilled bread: pre-heat a chargrill pan for about 10 minutes so that it is really hot. Cut your chosen bread into fairly thick slices, then lay them on the chargrill pan. Turn over when they have got nice dark stripes (about 40 seconds if the pan is really hot) and repeat on the other side.

Scotch Eggs with Fresh Herbs
Makes 4

4 large eggs, plus 1 small egg, beaten

8 oz (225 g) good-quality pork sausagemeat or sausages

2 spring onions, finely chopped

1 teaspoon finely chopped fresh thyme

3 teaspoons snipped chives

1 tablespoon finely chopped fresh parsley

a little plain flour, seasoned with salt and freshly milled black pepper, for dusting and coating

2 oz (50 g) white breadcrumbs, lightly toasted

groundnut or other flavourless oil for frying

salt and freshly milled black pepper

Scotch eggs are marvellous for travellers or picnickers. Take some spring onions to go with them and, if you've got plates, some chutney.

Begin by hardboiling the large eggs by placing them in a saucepan and add enough water to cover them by about $\frac{1}{2}$ inch (1 cm). Bring the water up to simmering point and put a timer on for 7 minutes. Then cool them rapidly under cold, running water. Let the cold tap run over them for about a minute, then leave them in cold water till they're cool.

Next, mix the sausagemeat with the spring onions and herbs and season well. (If you're using sausages, just slit the skins lengthways and peel them off.) Then shell the cooled eggs and coat each one with some seasoned flour. Divide the sausagemeat into 4 portions and pat each piece out on a floured surface to a shape roughly 3 x 5 inches (7.5 x 13 cm).

Now place an egg in the centre of each piece and carefully gather up the sausagemeat to cover each egg completely. Seal the joins well, and smooth and pat into shape all over. Next, coat them one by one, first in the beaten egg and then thoroughly and evenly in the breadcrumbs. Now heat $1\frac{1}{2}$ inches (4 cm) of oil in a large, deep frying pan up to a temperature of 350-375°F (180-190°C). (If you don't have a thermometer, you can easily test the temperature by frying a small cube of bread – if it turns golden brown within a minute, the oil is hot enough.) Put the eggs into the oil and fry for 6-8 minutes, turning frequently, until they have turned a nice brown colour. Drain on crumpled baking parchment or greaseproof paper.

Rillettes de Tours
Serves 8 as a first course or light lunch

a 2 lb 8 oz (1.15 kg) piece of lean belly pork, trimmed (trimmed weight 2 lb/900 g)

8 oz (225 g) back pork fat

1 dessertspoon chopped fresh thyme

½ teaspoon ground mace

1 heaped teaspoon salt

2 cloves garlic, crushed

10 black peppercorns

10 juniper berries

4 fl oz (120 ml) dry white wine

salt and freshly milled black pepper

You will also need a 2 pint (1.2 litre) terrine or 2 lb (900 g) loaf tin, and some kitchen foil.

Pre-heat the oven to gas mark 1, 275°F (140°C).

This is famous around the Loire district of France and sold everywhere in charcuteries – sometimes in thick chunks from a large terrine or packed into little pots. I would recommend this for anyone who doesn't like liver pâtés.

With your sharpest knife, cut the pork lengthwise into long strips about 1 inch (2.5 cm) wide, then cut each strip again into smaller strips so you end up with pieces that are approximately ½ x ¾ inch (1 x 2 cm), and place these in a bowl. Cut the fat into small pieces too, and mix these in (the excess fat will help to keep the pork properly moist during the cooking process). Now add the thyme, mace, salt and garlic, along with the peppercorns and juniper berries (the last 2 both crushed in a pestle and mortar or with the back of a tablespoon), and mix everything together. Transfer the whole lot to the terrine or loaf tin and pour in the wine.

Mix everything around to distribute the flavours, cover the terrine or loaf tin with foil and place it in the centre of the oven and leave it there for 4 hours. After that, taste a piece of pork and add more salt (and pepper), if necessary. Now empty everything into a large sieve standing over a bowl and let all the fat drip through (press the meat gently to extract the fat). Leave the drained fat to cool and then transfer to the fridge for 20-30 minutes so that the jelly and fat separate.

Next, take a couple of forks and pull the strips of meat into shreds (sometimes it is pounded instead, but personally, I think it's worth persevering with the fork method). Then pack the rillettes lightly into the terrine or loaf tin (wash and dry it thoroughly first), and leave to get cold. After that, remove the jelly from the bowl of fat, melt it gently and pour it over the rillettes. Then spread a layer of fat over the top to keep the meat moist. Keep the rillettes in the fridge (covered with foil or clingfilm) till needed; it will take about 2 hours to set. Serve with hot toast, crusty bread or crisp baked croutons.

Spiced Pork Kebabs with Apricots
Serves 2

1 lb (450 g) shoulder or leg of pork, cut into 1 inch (2.5 cm) cubes

2 oz (50 g) ready-to-eat dried apricots

1 tablespoon groundnut or other flavourless oil

1 small onion, chopped small

1 small clove garlic, crushed

1 heaped teaspoon ground ginger

1 heaped teaspoon ground turmeric

1 heaped tablespoon medium curry powder

2 tablespoons lemon juice

1 bay leaf

1 tablespoon light soft brown sugar

5 fl oz (150 ml) vegetable stock

salt and freshly milled black pepper

You will also need 4 wooden bamboo skewers, 10 inches (25.5 cm) long. Alternatively, use metal skewers.

Needless to say you use dried apricots for this pleasantly spicy dish, and although it is simple, you do need to leave time to make it, because the pork should marinade for several hours before cooking.

First, cover the dried apricots with cold water in a pan and bring them up to the boil, then simmer them gently for 15 minutes or until soft. After that, drain the apricots, reserving 3 tablespoons of the soaking water, and then whiz them with the water in a food processor until smooth.

Next, heat the oil in a large saucepan, add the onion and garlic and cook gently to soften for 10 minutes. Then add the ground ginger, turmeric and curry powder and cook for a further 2 minutes, followed by the puréed apricots, lemon juice, bay leaf and sugar. Pour in the stock and stir to amalgamate everything. Finally, add a seasoning of salt and pepper, then leave to cool. When cold, put the marinade and cubes of pork in a bowl, stir to get them well coated, then cover and leave them to marinate in a cool place for 3-4 hours.

If you are using wooden skewers you need to soak them for 30 minutes in hot water before cooking (to prevent them burning). Then when you're ready to cook the pork, pre-heat the grill for 10 minutes to its highest setting and set the grill tray 4 inches (10 cm) from the element. Next, thread the cubes of pork on to skewers. Grill the pork – not too near the heat – for 20-25 minutes, turning them halfway, until cooked and golden brown.

Meanwhile, reheat the leftover apricot marinade in a pan, simmer gently for a couple of minutes, then serve the pork kebabs with spiced basmati rice and the marinade.

Pork and Apple Rissoles with Spiced Apple Sauce
Serves 4

For the rissoles

1 lb (450 g) minced leftover cooked pork, or raw minced pork (not too lean)

1 medium (8 oz/225 g) Bramley cooking apple, peeled, cored and quartered

1 medium onion, peeled and quartered

4 oz (110 g) fresh white breadcrumbs

1 heaped dessertspoon chopped fresh sage

¼ teaspoon ground mace

1 teaspoon salt

groundnut or other flavourless oil, for frying

freshly milled black pepper

For the sauce

1 medium (8 oz/225 g) Bramley cooking apple, peeled, cored and chopped

½ small onion, peeled and thinly sliced

1 oz (25 g) butter

freshly grated nutmeg

a couple of pinches of ground cloves

1 dessertspoon caster sugar, or more, to taste

These can be made with leftover cooked pork from a joint or the ready minced raw pork which is now widely available.

To make the rissoles, all you do is place the onion, breadcrumbs, apple, sage, mace, salt and some freshly milled black pepper into the bowl of a processor and blend everything on a low speed, then add the pork and blend again until everything is thoroughly mixed. If you don't have a processor, grate the onion and apple and mix the ingredients together with a fork. Now divide the mixture into 16 and shape into rounds so you end up with 16 rissoles. All this can be done in advance, and the rissoles can be covered and chilled in the fridge.

Meanwhile, to make the sauce, soften the onion in the butter for 8-10 minutes, then stir in the chopped apple and 1 tablespoon water. Put a lid on and simmer for 8-10 minutes or until the apple is soft, then add a little freshly grated nutmeg, a couple of small pinches of ground cloves and the sugar. Beat the sauce till fluffy and taste to see if it needs a little more sugar.

When you're ready to cook the rissoles, heat some oil in a large frying pan (just enough to cover the base) and, when it's very hot, fry the rissoles in 2 batches for about 5 minutes on each side (if you're using raw pork, they will need 6-7 minutes). Serve the spiced apple sauce hot with the rissoles.

Old-fashioned Raised Pork Pies
Makes 6

For the filling

12 oz (350 g) pork shoulder, including some fat

4 oz (110 g) unsmoked back bacon rashers, derinded

1 heaped teaspoon chopped fresh sage

½ teaspoon anchovy essence

¼ teaspoon ground allspice

¼ teaspoon ground mace

salt and freshly milled black pepper

For the hot-water crust pastry

8 oz (225 g) strong plain white flour, plus a little extra for dusting

a pinch of salt

1 fl oz (25 ml) milk

3 oz (75 g) lard

To glaze

1 large egg yolk

You will also need a non-stick muffin tin, with 6 cups, each one 3 inches (7.5 cm) across the top, and about 1¼ inches (3 cm) deep, lightly buttered, a plain 3¼ inch (8 cm) pastry cutter, and a baking sheet.

These were originally raised by hand using old-fashioned wooden pie moulds but, in the 21st century, deep muffin tins make everything so much simpler. The most famous English pork pies come from Melton Mowbray and traditionally, a very small amount of anchovy essence was used to add subtle additional flavour.

Begin the recipe by preparing the meats which need to be coarsely chopped in a processor using the pulse button – you need a chopped rather than a minced effect. Then simply combine all the filling ingredients and give everything a really good seasoning. Pre-heat the oven to gas mark 4, 350°F (180°C).

Next, the pastry: sift the flour and salt into a bowl and then put the milk and 1 fl oz (25 ml) of water into a small saucepan and add the lard, cut up into small pieces. Place the pan over a gentle heat and when the fat has completely melted in the liquid, turn up the heat to bring it just up to the boil, and pour it on to the flour and, using a wooden spoon, mix everything together.

Turn the dough out on to a working surface and knead very lightly and briefly. You have to work quickly now, as it's important that the pies go into the tin while the dough is still warm. Take two-thirds of the dough and cut this up into 6 equal parts. Roll each of these into a ball and put 1 into each of the holes in the tin. Using your thumb, quickly press each ball flat on to the base and then up to the top edge. Press the pastry over the rim of the top edge, it should overlap by at least ¼ inch (5 mm).

Now divide the processed pork mixture among the lined muffin cups. Then roll out the remaining pastry and cut out six 3¼ inch (8 cm) rounds for lids; the pastry will be quite thin, so you may need to sprinkle the work surface with a little flour.

Next, using a pastry brush, paint a little egg yolk round the edge of each lid and gently press a lid on each pie, egg side down. Then, using a small fork, press the rims of the lids against the tops of the pie cases. Re-roll any pastry trimmings and cut out diamond-shaped leaves to decorate the lids. Then glaze the tops of the pies with the rest of the egg yolk and make a steam hole in each one. Now place the muffin tin on the baking sheet and bake the pies for 30 minutes on the middle shelf, then remove them from the oven. After this time, carefully and, using a small, round-bladed knife and oven gloves (or a thick cloth), remove the hot pies from the tin and place them directly on to the hot baking sheet; this will make the sides and base crispy.

Bake for a further 20-25 minutes or until the sides and base of the pies are crispy, then leave them to cool on a wire rack.

Conversions for Australia and New Zealand

Measurements in this book refer to British standard imperial and metric measurements.

The standard UK teaspoon measure is 5 ml, the dessertspoon is 10 ml and the tablespoon measure is 15 ml. In Australia, the standard tablespoon is 20 ml.

UK large eggs weigh 63-73 g.

Converting standard cups to imperial and metric weights

Ingredients (1 cup)	Imperial/metric
borlotti beans, dried	7 oz/200 g
breadcrumbs, fresh	3 oz/75 g
butter	9 oz/250 g
cannellini beans, dried	7 oz/200 g
flour, plain	4½ oz/125 g
haricot beans, dried	7 oz/200 g
lard	9 oz/250 g
lentils, Puy	7 oz/200 g
marrowfat peas, dried	7 oz/200 g
olives, unpitted	6 oz/175 g
prunes, whole, pitted	7½ oz/210 g
raisins	4½ oz/125 g
shredded suet	4½ oz/125 g
split peas, green	7 oz/200 g
sugar, golden caster	9 oz/250 g
sugar, soft brown*	8¼ oz/230 g

*Firmly packed

Liquid cup conversions

Imperial	Metric	Cups
1 fl oz	25 ml	⅛ cup
2 fl oz	55 ml	¼ cup
2¾ fl oz	70 ml	⅓ cup
4 fl oz	120 ml	½ cup
6 fl oz	175 ml	¾ cup
8 fl oz	225 ml	1 cup
10 fl oz	275 ml	1¼ cups
12 fl oz	340 ml	1½ cups
16 fl oz	450 ml	2 cups
1 pint	570 ml	2½ cups
24 fl oz	680 ml	3 cups
32 fl oz	1 litre	4 cups

A few ingredient names

Agen prunes, pitted
large ready-to-eat prunes

Bramley apples
green cooking apples

Cheshire cheese
crumbly-textured hard cheese

chestnut mushrooms
small brown mushrooms

Cox's apples
small dessert apples

Desirée potatoes
waxy, fleshed potatoes

double cream
thick cream

golden caster sugar
if unavailable, use caster sugar

open-cap/dark-gilled mushrooms
if unavailable, use flat-cap mushrooms

pepper, red
capsicum

shallots
eschalot/French shallots

single cream
thin cream

spinach
English spinach

spring onions
salad onions/shallots

streaky bacon
if unavailable, use sliced pancetta or speck

tomato purée
tomato paste

Index

Miki Duisterhof 6, 10, 38, 48, 68, 81,
93, 96, 102, 121, 133
Norman Hollands 6, 59, 72, 102, 114
Peter Knab 6, 15, 16, 19, 23, 42, 44,
47, 67, 72, 75, 94/95, 102, 122
Jonathan Lovekin 24, 44
J P Masclet 137
Michael Paul 9, 27, 28, 31, 41, 44, 56,
60, 63, 72, 82, 99, 105, 110, 117, 118,
126, 131
Simon Smith 35, 100
Petrina Tinslay 89
Simon Walton 6, 20, 24, 44, 52, 55, 59,
71, 72, 78, 81, 85, 90, 102, 109, 114,
125, 129
Cameron Watt 6, 12/13, 32, 36/37, 44,
51, 64/65, 72, 76/77, 86, 106, 112/113
Rob White 72

Delia Smith is Britain's best-selling cookery author, whose books have sold over 16 million copies.

Delia's other books include *How To Cook Books One*, *Two* and *Three*, *The Delia Collection: Soup*, *Chicken*, *Fish*, *Italian* and *Chocolate*, her *Vegetarian Collection*, the *Complete Illustrated Cookery Course*, *One Is Fun*, the *Summer* and *Winter Collections* and *Christmas*. She has launched her own website. She is also a director of Norwich City Football Club, where she is in charge of Canary Catering, several restaurants and a regular series of food and wine workshops.

She is married to the writer and editor Michael Wynn Jones and they live in Suffolk.

For more information on Delia's restaurant,
food and wine workshops and events, contact:
Delia's Canary Catering, Norwich City Football Club, Carrow Road,
Norwich NR1 1JE; www.deliascanarycatering.co.uk
For Delia's Canary Catering (conferencing and events enquiries),
telephone 01603 218704
For Delia's Restaurant and Bar (reservations),
telephone 01603 218705

Visit Delia's website at www.deliaonline.com